Your Clothes Say It for You

Your Clothes Say It for You

By

Elizabeth Rice Handford

SWORD of the LORD
PUBLISHERS
P. O. BOX 1099, MURFREESBORO, TN 37133

Printed and Bound in the United States of America

Contents

Before you turn the page. . .

May I have a word with you?

This book is about a very controversial subject. We women don't really like to be told what to wear. The only reason I dare write on the subject is that there are women who earnestly wish to please God. They would do what God wants them to do about their appearance, if only they knew what He wanted. It is for these honest, open-minded women who want to please God that I write.

I went to a meeting of Christians where demure Mennonite women in somber, floor-length dresses and white caps sat next to women in pantsuits. Other women, carefully and tastefully dressed, sat by barefoot girls with bare midriffs, wearing blue jeans (one with the surprising words, "Smile, God loves you," printed on the seat!). These women would have agreed that the Bible really is the Word of God. Why then were their dress standards so very different?

Are there clear standards in the Word of God for the way we clothe ourselves? When our children complain about our standards for their clothing, do we have any plain instruction from the Bible for them? Is it disobedience for a woman to wear slacks? Are we accountable for the Scripture that commands women to wear their hair long? Does it really make any difference at all to God about what a woman wears?

You have an opinion about all this. Is it based on the Bible? Are you willing to consider what the Scriptures say? Will you make a decision, not by what is convenient, not by what others are wearing, but simply by the Word of God?

The Bible tells us that if we are willing to *do* God's will we can *know* God's will (John 7:17). You can know what God requires, if you are willing to do whatever He says.

God does have a standard for your appearance. If you are ready to find out what it is, then I invite you to turn the page.

Chapter 1

Does It Matter to God How You Dress?

They lived in Paradise, the man and his wife. Nothing their heart could desire had been denied them. Their days were filled with new discoveries and sweet delight. The whole of God's wonderful creation was theirs to enjoy. In the cool of the day, God Himself, the One who inhabits eternity, came down to walk and talk with them.

But one evening when God sought fellowship with His creatures, they were not there to greet Him. Never before had He had to call them.

"Adam, where art thou? . . . Adam? . . . Adam!"

Adam stepped from the shadows of the woods where he had hidden. Before he uttered a word, his garments betrayed what had happened. His pitiful, withered fig leaves, stitched together with twigs, plainly said Adam had tasted the forbidden fruit!

"I heard thy voice in the garden," Adam said in a low voice, his eyes downcast. "I was afraid, because I was naked, and I hid myself." As he spoke, he trembled. The dried fig leaves rustled and crumbled. When he clutched at them, they shredded even more.

In a voice somber with grief, God asked, "Who told thee that thou wast naked? Hast thou eaten of the tree, whereof I commanded thee that thou shouldest not eat?" (Gen. 3:11). God knew the answer to that question and had known from ages past the choices His creatures would make. Indeed, God the Father had already covenanted with God the Son, the means of their redemption. But His foreknowledge could not lessen the pain that must have wrenched His great heart when Adam spoke those doomed words: "The woman . . . gave me of the tree, and I did eat."

Then God slaughtered innocent animals. He took their skins, cleaned them and cured them (Gen. 3:21). Then that holy God stitched those skins into covering garments for His children, and His fingers were drenched with His tears as He stitched.

That day death settled down on the earth like a fever-laden fog. Its ravages would never be halted except by the death of the One who is Life.

This Scripture tells us God was deeply concerned about the clothing of Adam and Eve. It is reasonable to assume that our clothing is also His concern. From this Genesis account, we can draw the principles by which we ought to clothe ourselves.

First notice that Adam and Eve's clothing betrayed their spiritual condition. When they were innocent of sin, they had no clothing and were not aware of any lack (Gen. 2:25). Later, their crumbling fig leaves betrayed the fact they had sinned.

The fig leaves prompted God's question, "Hast thou eaten of the tree, whereof I commanded thee that thou shouldest not eat?" Their clothing revealed they were sinners. Then God clothed them in durable garments of soft suede, thereby picturing the death of Christ who would clothe us with His robe of righteousness (Isa. 61:10). That clothing testified that they were forgiven, covered sinners.

So, it seems, our clothing reveals something of our spiritual condition.

Second, we can infer from this Scripture that, after the Fall, Adam and Eve became aware of their innate maleness and femaleness. In the perfect creation, Adam and Eve seem to have been conscious of their oneness, not their differentness: "This is now bone of my bones, and flesh of my flesh. . . and they shall be one flesh" (Gen. 2:23, 24). Not until after the Fall were their "eyes . . . opened, and they knew that they were naked" (Gen. 3:7).

God has built into human consciousness an innate awareness of the distinctiveness of men and women. This affects the commands He gives concerning clothing.

Third, we can observe that in God's perfect creation, Adam and Eve felt no need to cover their bodies. But in the ruined chaos of the world after the Fall, they knew instinctively that they must be covered. Before sin entered the world, there was no temptation, no sin in viewing the unclothed, naked body. But when sin came, those beautiful bodies, created in honor and glory in the image of God, were subjected to dishonor and weakness (I Cor. 15:43). The act of love, designed by God to be holy and sublime, was now mimicked by lustful, unholy desires Satan would use to induce people to sin.

Because we are sinners, subject to the temptations of sinners, it is needful to clothe our bodies.

These three truths can help us decide how God wants us to dress. Let's talk about each of them further.

Chapter 2

Whose Team Are You On?

Even if you missed the first half of the old TV westerns, you knew who was who. The good guy wore white—a white cowboy hat, and he rode a white horse. When he went into the saloon he always, to the bartender's astonishment, ordered a glass of milk.

You always knew who the villain was, too. He sported a black hat, twirled a black mustache, and rode a black horse.

Why did sophisticated TV viewers put up with such transparent type-casting? Because there is an elemental truth: what you wear speaks for you. Your appearance tells people whose team you are on.

When you go to a football game, you know who is on your team because he wears your team's uniform. In a similar sense, you wear a uniform daily, and it tells people whose team you are on.

Remember the rebels of the '60s? They wore a distinct uniform, usually faded blue jeans with frayed edges. They wore unkempt beards. They wouldn't wash their hair or use deodorant. They stitched the United States flag upside down on their sleeves. What were they saying? "I don't like the standards of the establishment. I hate everything you cherish. My clothing shows my contempt for you!"

Down through the decades, dissident groups have shown their hostility in the clothing they choose.

Another "for instance": a young wife knows her husband will be home for supper at 6:00. While supper bubbles on the stove, she sets the table with real silver and lights the candles. Then she hurries to put on a fresh dress and a whiff of perfume.

When her young husband walks in the door, she doesn't need to say a word. He knows at a glance that she is saying,

"I love you. You are important to me. I'm so glad you are home."

We daily assess people—rightly or wrongly—by what they wear.

I would find it difficult to trust a banker with greasy long hair who wore a denim shirt with a stained collar, even if my deposit was insured by the United States government.

A doctor often knows when a female patient is getting better, for she starts caring again about her appearance.

We tend to think a waitress with bleached hair, skimpy skirt and exposed bosom probably offers more than the noon lunch special.

We may err in our judgment of the outside. We may make a wrong decision about what the person is really like on the inside. Nevertheless, we do judge people by how they dress, and probably have some foundation for doing so.

For several years I acted as principal of our church's Christian day school. Sometimes a parent would come to enroll a child and say, "This child has just been expelled from another school. It wasn't really his fault. He accidentally got in with the wrong crowd. If you'll accept him here, he won't have any problems in this good Christian atmosphere."

If I let compassion overwhelm good judgment and accepted the "misguided" student, I often found that by noon of his first day in school he had found his niche with the school rebels. He had aligned himself with the malcontents.

How did they find each other so quickly? How did they identify themselves? I never knew. It wasn't simply their clothing: every child had to conform to school rules of hairstyle and dress. It was something much more subtle. In some mysterious way, their appearance identified them.

Whose team are you on? Do you love the Lord Jesus? Do you want to be known as His follower? Does your clothing line you up with Him?

Chapter 3

God Wants You to Be Beautiful

God loves beautiful things. His whole creation, damaged though it now is, still breathes the grace and passion of the One who delights in creating beautiful things. Our minds leap, when we think of God's beautiful creation, to the flowers He made, their multitudinous variety of color and form, the perfection of each tiny pistil and stamen, the fragrance wafting from each.

But the same infinite gamut of design may be found in a thousand different areas of creation, each just as great in variety: fish and birds, mountains and minerals, seasons, storms and seas, mighty jungle beasts and microscopic one-celled organisms, stars, snowflakes and atoms. They are all beautiful. They all speak of a Creator who delighted in fashioning their form and function, their design and craft.

"He hath made every thing beautiful in his time," the wise king said in Ecclesiastes 3:11. His creation reflects the Creator, the One who is "the Father of lights," the giver of every good and perfect gift (Jas. 1:17).

Why does the human heart long for beauty? Because it longs for God. David prayed, "One thing have I desired of the Lord, that will I seek after; that I may dwell in the house of the Lord all the days of my life, to behold the beauty of the Lord, and to enquire in his temple" (Ps. 27:4).

When God made us, He created us in His image. "He hath made every thing beautiful in his time," Ecclesiastes 3:11 says; "also he hath set the world in their heart." The word *"world"* here means "eternity." God created us with a longing for the eternally beautiful things.

God spent a great deal of time giving Moses explicit instructions for making the priests' garments in Exodus 28. He directed the colors, the fabrics, the design and the pattern of the embroidery (vss. 5, 32). Why? ". . . for glory and for beauty" (vs. 40).

The virtuous woman in Proverbs 31 spent her time not just in clothing her children, but making their clothing pretty.

"She is not afraid of the snow for her household: for all her household are clothed with scarlet. She maketh herself coverings of tapestry; her clothing is silk and purple."— Vss. 21,22.

The Scriptures frequently mention the bride adorned for her husband (Isa. 49:18; 61:10; Jer. 2:32; Rev. 21:2). Naomi instructed Ruth, her daughter-in-law, just how she was to prepare herself for her encounter with Boaz, and it included careful anointing and adorning (Ruth 3:3).

One of the most poignant parables in all Scripture is found in Ezekiel 16. Walking through a field, a man found a newborn baby girl abandoned by her mother. Unwashed, bloody, pitied by none, the child would have perished but for the compassion of the stranger who happened by.

He picked up that tiny body, brought her to his house, and whispered in her ear, 'Live! Oh, please live!' And she did live, sustained by his love.

The years went by, God says in the parable. She grew up into a lovely young woman. "Thy time was the time of love," he said, so he covenanted himself to be her husband. Ezekiel 16 tells us what he did for the girl he was to marry:

"I clothed thee also with broidered work, and shod thee with badgers' skin, and I girded thee about with fine linen, and I covered thee with silk.

"I decked thee also with ornaments, and I put bracelets upon thy hands, and a chain on thy neck.

"And I put a jewel on thy forehead, and earrings in thine ears, and a beautiful crown upon thine head.

"Thus wast thou decked with gold and silver; and thy raiment was of fine linen, and silk, and broidered work; thou didst eat fine flour, and honey, and oil: and thou wast exceeding beautiful, and thou didst prosper into a kingdom.

"And thy renown went forth among the heathen for thy beauty: for it was perfect through my comeliness, which I had put upon thee, saith the Lord God."—Ezek. 16:10–14.

Every beautiful ornament that could be imagined was prepared by the man getting his bride ready for her wedding. And since this man pictures the Lord Jesus, who by His death clothed us and made us ready for His heavenly Home (Eph. 5:25–27), it is safe to assume God Himself takes pleasure in a woman's adorning herself for her husband.

When God called the children of Israel to meet Him at Mount Sinai to give them the Law, He commanded Moses:

"Go unto the people, and sanctify them to day and to morrow, and let them wash their clothes, And be ready against the third day: for the third day the Lord will come down in the sight of all the people upon mount Sinai."—Exod. 19:10,11.

God wanted His people clean in body and dress when they met Him.

When God gave instructions to Moses about constructing the Tabernacle, He told him to make a laver of brass where the priests could wash before going in to make a sacrifice (Exod. 30:17–20). If they failed to wash, they died.

Priests were not to wear any garment that would cause them to sweat in the presence of God. Wool was expressly forbidden (Ezek. 44:17,18).

These Scriptures all tell us that the Lord loves beautiful things. When we dress to show we are on God's side, we can be sure that does not mean we deliberately should make ourselves ugly.

God is disgusted when people try to make themselves appear spiritual by looking ugly. The Pharisees would not wash their faces, would not comb their hair, and would wear a sad countenance so everyone would know they were fasting—that is, being "spiritual."

Jesus called them hypocrites. He wanted them to groom

themselves better when fasting so others wouldn't know. "Thou, when thou fastest, anoint thine head, and wash thy face; That thou appear not unto men to fast, but unto thy Father which is in secret" (Matt. 6:17,18).

Don't mistake it: our piety is not shown by how dirty we are.

It does not honor the Lord for a woman to let her hair straggle in lumpy, oily coils, or allow her slip to show ragged, trailing lace.   Unpolished shoes with run-down heels and hose with runs don't honor the Lord. A shapeless, wrinkled dress over an obese body doesn't prove a woman loves God. It more likely proves she loves fleshly things and that she is lazy and undisciplined.

The Christian's body is the temple of the Holy Spirit (I Cor. 6:19,20). We dishonor Him when we abuse His temple.

When a godly woman wants her appearance to show she belongs to the Lord, she'll keep her hair gleaming clean and neat. Her fingernails will be trimmed and clean. She'll use underarm deodorant and a razor when it's needed. She'll brush her teeth (and see her dentist twice a year, as the TV commercial says) and make sure her breath is sweet.

Her complexion will be as clear and fresh as a healthy diet and soap and water can make it.

Her clothing will be clean and wrinkle-free, well-fitting and suitable. After all, she's a princess, a daughter of the King of kings, and her appearance ought to honor Him.

Some have felt that the Scripture in I Timothy 2:9,10 forbids the wearing of any jewelry or the styling of the hair, since it says a woman is to adorn herself "not with broided hair, or gold, or pearls, or costly array." First Peter 3:3 says, "Whose adorning let it not be that outward adorning of plaiting the hair, and of wearing of gold, or of putting on of apparel."

But these Scriptures are not forbidding the wearing of jewelry or the styling of hair; they are saying a woman must not depend on them for her adornment. If we believe this forbids ornamentation of any kind, then we are driven to the foolish position that the I Peter 3 passage forbids the wearing of clothing at all! That obviously is not the intent of these Scriptures. The emphasis here is that the adorning must come from within, from the spirit, which is not subject to corruption.

Of course, it is possible to spend too much time and attention on your appearance, and that could lead to sin.

Remember the husband, in Ezekiel 16, who prepared his bride for marriage? The end of that parable is unbelievably sad. His wife took his loving bridal gifts and used them to attract lovers.

She took the beautifully-colored garments and spread them on her harlot's bed. She took his jewels of gold and silver and fashioned them into idols. The children born of her harlotry she burned in sacrifice to her idols (Ezek. 16:15–21).

In this case, beyond the shadow of doubt, her womanly ornaments became a curse instead of an adornment.

In fact, many Scriptures describe a woman adorning herself for the specific purpose of luring a man into sin.

Hosea's wife decked herself with earrings and jewels to attract lovers (Hos. 2:13).

Tamar, the daughter-in-law of Judah, setting out to seduce him, put on "harlot's attire" (Gen. 38:14,15).

Isaiah, chapter 3, tells of the time "when Jerusalem is ruined, and Judah is fallen." Yet some women living then seemed untouched by the awful condition of their country. They dressed themselves with:

"Tinkling ornaments about their feet, and their cauls [headbands], *and their round tires* [necklaces] *like the moon,*

"The chains, and the bracelets, and the mufflers,

"The bonnets, and the ornaments of the legs, and the headbands, and the tablets [perfume bottles], *and the earrings,*

"The rings, and nose jewels, The changeable suits of apparel, and the mantles, and the wimples, and the crisping pins,

"The glasses [mirrors], *and the fine linen, and the hoods* [tiaras], *and the vails."*—Isa. 3:18–23.

What an assortment of devices these wicked women used to curl their hair and adorn themselves!

God was indignant with these women who spent all their time and energy on their appearance when issues of life and death were before them. His judgment was: "And it shall come to pass, that instead of sweet smell there shall be stink; and instead of a girdle a rent; and instead of well set hair baldness; and instead of a stomacher a girding of sackcloth; and burning instead of beauty" (Isa. 3:24).

It is wrong to be concerned about temporal things to the neglect of eternal matters!

God said to the women of Israel, as Nebuchadnezzar's army crouched at the city gates: "And when thou art spoiled, what wilt thou do? Though thou clothest thyself with crimson, though thou deckest thee with ornaments of gold, though thou rentest thy face with painting, in vain shalt thou make thyself fair; thy lovers will despise thee, they will seek thy life" (Jer. 4:30).

Queen Jezebel, wife of Ahab, king of Israel, was an exceedingly wicked woman. "There was none like unto Ahab, which did sell himself to work wickedness in the sight of the Lord," I Kings 21:25 says. Then it adds this terrible statement: "whom Jezebel his wife stirred up."

A man named Jehu set out to avenge the sins Jezebel had committed. Jezebel prepared for his coming by 'painting her face and tiring her head [arranging her hair]' (II Kings 9:30).

What was her intent, at that time of judgment, in adorning herself? Was it to distract, perhaps seduce, God's messenger? Or was she so warped by her wickedness that it didn't occur to her to worry about anything but her physical

attractiveness? Whatever her reason, it did not prevent her bloody and terrible death.

On the other hand, people who are suddenly convicted of their sin in the presence of God seem to lose their concern about their physical appearance. The children of Israel fell into great sin and worshipped the golden calf while Moses was on Mount Sinai. When they came to realize the awfulness of their sin, Exodus 33:4–6 tells us they stripped themselves of their ornaments and mourned.

Men seeking God's favor and convicted of sin often dressed in the rough garments of sackcloth. Mordecai wore sackcloth when he heard of Haman's wicked plan to kill the Jews (Esther 4:1). Daniel, when he was fasting because of his people's sins, put on sackcloth and ashes (Dan. 9:3). Another time he did not anoint himself for three whole weeks because he was so intent on getting God's mercy (Dan. 10:3).

When Elisha the prophet healed Naaman of his leprosy, Naaman wanted to give him beautiful, expensive garments. Elisha refused the gifts, but his servant Gehazi determined to own them for himself. When he came back with the garments, gained by a lie, Elisha said to Gehazi, "Is it a time to receive money, and to receive garments?" (II Kings 5:26). His punishment for coveting the garments and lying to get them was leprosy!

Too much care for the externals, too much concern for the adornment and comfort of the body, can lead to sin.

In recent years many teenagers have started wearing tacky, "grungy" clothing. Their clothes aren't simply casual; they are positively sloppy. Some buy faded denim jeans with pre-cut holes in the knee (the sign in the department store proclaimed "pre-faded, pre-frayed jeans"—and the price was exactly double that of ordinary jeans). They put together "poor boy" outfits.

Is a trend toward ugly clothing a sincere desire to get back to unmaterialistic values? I think perhaps it is not. Teens say that by wearing this kind of clothing they are protesting their parents' materialistic values. (And, face it, many of their parents are materialistic.)

But the fact that such "mod" clothing costs measurably more than conventional clothing makes me question their motives, especially when the teen is willing to let the harassed, materialistic parent pay for it! The truth is, sometimes such clothing actually says, "I reject the authority of my parents."

Where is the balance? How can we know what is too little, too much? How should we dress to make sure people looking at us know we love the Lord?

Chapter 4

God Wants Moderation in Your Clothing

In the late '70s, our son John earned his way through college by working in the auto repair shop of a large retail chain. He was given a bulletin from the store manager that said:

Subject: Current Dress Code

Since fashion is constantly changing and there is more and more variety of clothes for both men and women, hard-and-fast rules or codes for dress are difficult to develop, and sometimes the "right" clothes can be a matter of an individual's taste.

The best way to describe our "code" is that extremes in anything are generally out, as well as any clothes, hair, shoes, or accessories that would make our store look like a scene from the beach, a resort, a ballroom, or a dude ranch.

Those things would include hot pants, culottes, jeans, slacks and sweaters, gauchos and knickers, floor-length skirts, jump-suits, bare midriffs, string-straps or bra dresses; and jeans, turtlenecks, and other sport apparel for men. Anything else extreme, like extremely long hair or unkempt beards for men or hats or elaborate accessories for women, detract from a store's professional appearance.

Someone once said, "It's easier to get where you'd like to be if you dress like you're already there." People tend to present a total image, not only by how they act and what they do, but how they look. Dressing with dignity as well as style and flair just may hasten your trip to success.

(Signed) The Store Manager

Perhaps some of the styles mentioned would now be accepted in that same chain, but the manager's principle of moderation is a good biblical principle.

Moderation in clothing is taught especially in I Timothy 2:9 and 15. Verse 9 says, "In like manner also, that women adorn themselves in modest apparel, with shamefacedness and sobriety." Verse 15 says, "Continue in faith and charity and holiness with sobriety." The word "sobriety" in these two verses is the Greek word sophrosune. It means "prudence" or "moderation." Women are to clothe themselves in modest apparel with moderation.

The English word moderation is used in Philippians 4:5: "Let your moderation be known unto all men." Here the Greek word gives the idea of gentleness and patience rather than an aggressive attitude.

Why ought we to let our moderation be known to all? Because "the Lord is at hand," or "nigh." The presence of the Lord Jesus pressures us to keep important things important and unimportant things in their place.

Jesus is coming back for His redeemed. When we face Him, we'll be ashamed if we have let a temporal thing like clothing control our lives. So a woman ought to dress with moderation.

In I Corinthians 9:19, Paul says that though he is "free from all men," he made himself servant to all so he could win as many as possible. His whole aim in life was to get as many people to Heaven as possible. In verse 25 he says, "And every man that striveth for the mastery is temperate in all things."

One who has the supreme goal of reaching people for Christ will be temperate in everything, including the place of clothing in his life. The word "temperate" means to exercise self-restraint, to put curbs on one's self.

This temperance is a fruit of the Spirit (Gal. 5:22,23). You don't "work it up." It comes with letting the Holy Spirit control your heart and actions. God expects us to develop it

(II Pet. 1:5), so hard self-discipline is required.

Paul said in I Corinthians 9:27, "I keep under my body, and bring it into subjection: lest that by any means, when I have preached to others, I myself should be a castaway."

An earnest Christian woman will keep her body, the external, subject to the Spirit and make it her servant rather than letting it master her.

In Titus 2:5 women are commanded to be "discreet." That Greek word is related to the word *"sobriety"* in I Timothy, chapter 2. It means, "Of sound mind, taste, discretion, sense."

Christian women are to be discreet; they are to have good taste and good sense. Surely this should be true of how a woman dresses.

Proverbs 11:22 complains that 'a fair woman without discretion is like a jewel in a swine's snout.' Can you visualize a big, fat, dirty sow, wallowing and grunting in the mud with an exquisite diamond in her nose? A naturally beautiful woman who lacks discretion is as painfully distasteful.

Occasionally we women have put up with clothes that were really uncomfortable or in poor taste only because a designer somewhere decreed them fashionable.

Remember those huge block heels on shoes that made us galumph like a hippopotamus? Then there were the shoes with toes so narrow that some foolish women had their little toes surgically removed so they could be "stylish"! How often have we endured awkward styles because a designer, looking for something new, ignored good taste and artistic sense!

I suppose the problem comes as we try to determine what is aesthetic and what is moral principle.

Of course a woman, liking pretty things as she does, wants new styles in jewelry and clothing. It's exciting to see the inventive human mind apply itself to feminine adornment and think of ingenious ways to decorate clothing.

We would be bored if we had to wear the same skirt style, the same sleeve length, a collar cut the same way, all the time. The essence of good fashion design is to find fresh and pretty ways to drape the female frame.

But a woman's choice of clothing must still be governed by God's command for moderation: "modest apparel, with shamefacedness and sobriety; not with broided hair, or gold, or pearls, or costly array" (I Tim. 2:9). To break this command exposes a woman to serious temptation. She will be vulnerable to Satan's snares if she is too absorbed in her body and its adornment.

Our children need to be taught the importance of this principle. In their teen years especially, children want to look like, and have the approval of, their classmates. Mother may say, "You look very nice, dear," but what really matters is "What will the kids at school think?"

A child picking out frames for glasses at the optometrist's may think they are just right until one of the "in" crowd at school makes a sniping comment. Then the child is ready to scrap glasses forever and view the world with blurred vision.

Our children will pressure us to let them conform to the standards of the "in" group. A daughter wails, "But, Mother, all the girls in the sixth grade wear hose to school." When you investigate, you may find perhaps four girls do, and the rest of the girls are going to badger their parents until they can wear hose, too!

This is where a mother must be truly wise. Many youthful fads are a part of a child's expressing his differentness, his membership in "the club," or just personal taste.

If the silly socks, the bangles, the crazy cap, do not hurt the child, if they do not reveal a wrong attitude, if they do not distract the child from his duties, then surely there is no harm in letting him express himself. We parents impose so many decisions on children, surely we can permit them some freedom of choice.

If striped socks are the style, fine. If penny loafers are "out" and saddle oxfords are "in," then little Sally surely could decide which she wanted.

So they look old-fashioned to you? Just wait. Someday your grandchildren will snicker at the styles your children are choosing now, and you can all laugh together about the vagaries of fashion.

Perhaps a sixth-grade girl ought not regularly wear hose to school. She has so little time to be a little girl. She ought to be able to run and play freely during recess. Father ought not to have to spend extra dollars to keep her in hose for that.

Discretion, moderation, cost and suitability, along with the child's particular preferences, all bear weight in determining what our children wear.

Please understand, I am not advocating that you wear old-fashioned, unsuitable clothing to prove you are a Christian. Nor do I believe formal vs. casual clothing is the issue. The key, again, is moderation.

What about makeup? Some women feel they ought not to use any makeup, since often in the Bible the women who used it were wicked (Isa. 57:9; Jer. 4:30; II Kings 9:30; Ezek. 23:40; Rev. 18:12,13).

But we know that the use of cosmetics on the face for lubrication was quite common (Ps. 104:15; Ezek. 16:9). There are ample references to the use of perfumes, ointments, and powders by those who loved the Lord (Prov. 27:9; Song of Sol. 1:3; 3:6; 4:10; Esther 2:12).

Dr. Bob Jones, Sr., used to say, "If the barn door needs painting, paint it!"

Moderation is the key to the way a godly woman uses makeup.

Anything that draws undue attention to the external body could be called immoderate. The body is only the picture frame, the vehicle, the means, for the spirit. Its adornment should enhance the personality, not detract from it.

This is one of the reasons God tells women not to adorn themselves with "broided hair, or gold, or pearls, or costly array." True adornment comes from the spirit, not the body.

If a woman feels she needs a touch of color, it probably

ought to be a natural color. Eye makeup ought not to make you look as if you'd mildewed in the high humidity. Fingernails ought not to be garish. Whatever is used to make up for nature's deficiencies ought to look like nature put it there, not a color-blind fence painter!

It seems to me that eyebrows should be groomed to be neat, but the natural line ought not be changed radically by severe plucking.

How long should fingernails be? My girls love long, tapered nails, and they do look lovely. Here, perhaps, the rule ought to be "form follows function."

God made a woman's hands to serve. Anytime beauty becomes more important than service, beauty has become too important. Extremely long nails require constant protection (even from dish washing, to hear my gals explain, trying to keep their faces straight). It isn't possible to play the piano well or use a computer keyboard with speed if fingernails are too long.

So let function—what God made your hands for—determine form (how long the nails should be).

What about hair coloring? I do not know of any Scripture that forbids it. The Lord does give great honor to gray hair. "The glory of young men is their strength: and the beauty of old men is the gray head" (Prov. 20:29). "The hoary head is a crown of glory, if it be found in the way of righteousness" (Prov. 16:31). The Lord Jesus Himself is described in Revelation 1:14 as having white hair.

My hairdresser has some practical objections to hair coloring. She says dyes and tints are very hard on the hair. She points out that when God designed you, He coordinated the color of your complexion, your eyes and your hair.

Tinkering with His color scheme sometimes yields startling results. God says in Matthew 5:36 that we are not to swear by our head, since we can't make one hair white or black. We can't, permanently, and the growing-out process betrays the attempt.

All these practical decisions should be governed by God's command that women adorn themselves with moderation.

Perhaps our desire to cover gray hair comes from accepting the world's belief that to be young is to be beautiful. People of the world seem to believe that as long as they deny old age, feebleness and death, they can't be touched by them.

Of course this isn't true. Peace comes only as we accept our mortality as part of the price of sin and receive the promises of forgiveness and eternal life through Christ.

"Though our outward man perish, yet the inward man is renewed day by day. For our light affliction, which is but for a moment, worketh for us a far more exceeding and eternal weight of glory; While we look not at the things which are seen, but at the things which are not seen: for the things which are seen are temporal; but the things which are not seen are eternal."—II Cor. 4:16–18.

There is another important thought in the matter of following the world's fashions. When we slavishly follow a particular fashion just because it is the fashion, without regard to intrinsic beauty, it could become a temptation. Anything we do solely because others do it can lead to sin. We must not let our judgment be determined by what everyone else thinks.

When God sent Samuel to Bethlehem to find a king among the sons of Jesse, Samuel saw a tall, handsome lad and said, "Surely the Lord's anointed is before him" (I Sam. 16:6).

But God said no. "The Lord seeth not as man seeth; for man looketh on the outward appearance, but the Lord looketh on the heart" (I Sam. 16:7).

If everyone approves of a certain thing, the likelihood is that it is wrong. "That which is highly esteemed among men is abomination in the sight of God," Jesus said in Luke 16:15.

How can an unsaved person who rejects God's authority

and cherishes his sin possibly love the things of God? He can't. His preferences and standards will be warped by his rebellion against God.

If we let the opinions of others determine our clothing decisions, regardless of how foolish and uncomfortable they are, we leave ourselves open to temptation. "The fear of man bringeth a snare; but whoso putteth his trust in the Lord shall be safe" (Prov. 29:25).

Proverbs 28:21 says, "To have respect of persons [unfair partiality] is not good, for for a piece of bread that man will transgress."

If it matters inordinately to me what you think, then it won't be long until I lose my convictions. If I let your opinion affect me, against my good judgment, about my clothing, I might let your opinion affect me in other more serious decisions.

Our appearance is the outpost, the early warning defense system. If it cracks under the pressure of worldly opinion, we may find our convictions also crumbling.

Think about it: how often has a friend unintentionally telegraphed a backslidden condition by a radical new hair style or daring dress?

If we put on the uniform of the wrong team, we make ourselves vulnerable to Satan's snares. A Christian woman should dress with sobriety, with moderation.

Chapter 5

God Wants to Supply Your Clothing Needs

From all the Scriptures we've looked at, it is obvious that it matters to God how we dress. His is not an idle interest, not a careless edict laid down without regard to its effect on us. On the contrary, He cares very much about every need of His children. So He cares when you need clothing, and He intends to provide it if you are His child and if you will put His business first.

Jesus preached a marvelous sermon about it in Matthew 6:25–33:

"Take no thought for your life, what ye shall eat, or what ye shall drink; nor yet for your body, what ye shall put on. Is not the life more than meat, and the body than raiment?

"Behold the fowls of the air: for they sow not, neither do they reap, nor gather into barns; yet your heavenly Father feedeth them. Are ye not much better than they?

"Which of you by taking thought can add one cubit unto his stature?

"And why take ye thought for raiment? Consider the lilies of the field, how they grow; they toil not, neither do they spin:

"And yet I say unto you, That even Solomon in all his glory was not arrayed like one of these."

Then Jesus makes a sweet promise of His concern:

"Wherefore, if God so clothe the grass of the field, which to day is, and to morrow is cast into the oven, shall he not much more clothe you, O ye of little faith?

"Therefore take no thought, saying, What shall we eat? or, What shall we drink? or, Wherewithal shall we be clothed?

"(For after all these things do the Gentiles seek:) for your

heavenly Father knoweth that ye have need of all these things.

*"But seek ye first the kingdom of God, and his righteous-
ness; and all these things shall be added unto you."*

When God created you, He took upon Himself the
responsibility for supplying your needs. He first saw to it
that you could receive eternal life through the death of His
Son, and then He promised, beyond that, to supply every
single need that you could ever encounter.

Because this is true, we can lay aside our fret and worry
about our family's needs and concentrate on seeking God's
righteousness, bringing people to Him, and letting Him provide our physical needs.

The truth is, making a material thing like clothing of
such paramount importance is sure to lead to frustration.
The fleshly body cannot be satisfied, ever. When it hungers
and is fed, it still will hunger again. When it thirsts and
drinks, it will thirst again. So when the body is clothed, it
will yet desire more clothing.

Ecclesiastes 5:10 says, "He that loveth silver shall not be
satisfied with silver; nor he that loveth abundance with
increase: this is also vanity."

A famous billionaire was asked (he tells the story in his
autobiography), "How much more money must you have to
make you satisfied?"

His reply is tragic but awesomely true, "Just a little
bit more."

If you ask a woman who makes clothes her god, "How
many more furs and jewels, how many more shoes, how
many more evening dresses must you own to be happy?" the
reply will always be, "Just a few more."

Thank God, there is a better way! Instead of worrying
about where money is coming from for school shoes for the
kids, for a winter jacket for your husband or a new dress
for yourself, spend your thoughts and energies in serving

the Lord. Let Him do the taking care of you—He is so eager to do it!

"My God shall supply all your need according to his riches in glory by Christ Jesus" (Phil. 4:19). How many riches in Glory? Vast beyond all comprehension. And He will supply from that hoard every single need you have, if you will put Him first.

In fact, it is almost fun to go through the hardship just to see how wonderfully He provides!

My husband is a pastor. We have seven children. By the time we divide up his very adequate salary among tuition for Christian school, food, gas and all the other things that siphon money out of the family treasury, there isn't a lot left over for clothes. But the Lord always sends exactly what is needed at exactly the right time.

Perhaps it will be a gift of money designated for clothes for the children.

Or perhaps someone will knock on the parsonage door with an armful of clothes. "Will it embarrass you if I give you my son's outgrown clothing?" she timidly might ask.

The kids chortle with glee, too excited to be embarrassed. We eagerly paw through the box and find exactly what one of the children needed.

Or, often, the local department store will have a half-price sale on outfits for girls, with skirts that also just "happen" to be long enough for a willowy teenage daughter.

Years ago, when son John was four and Ruthie two, my husband held a revival in a rural community in Iowa. We rented an old farmhouse for the two weeks. It was so isolated that there was little I could do in the day to help with the revival.

Ruthie desperately needed a winter coat, and I had plenty of time to make her a coat. There was an old treadle sewing machine in the farmhouse, so I had the means to make it. But I had no way to get the twenty miles into town to buy fabric, and there was no money to buy fabric if I had been able to get to the store.

That morning I prayed, "Lord, I know this sounds like a dumb request. But someone somewhere in this community has some leftover scraps from a coat she's made. Ruthie's such a little girl, it wouldn't take much material to make a coat for her. Right now I have lots of time to sew. Later on, when I get home, You know I'll be too busy to sew much. Do You suppose You could take care of this for me?"

That afternoon a woman drove up into the farmyard. She pulled a package out of the car and thrust it into my hand. "My daughter just finished making a nylon pile coat for herself. There's enough material left over for you to make your little girl a coat, I think. Do you sew?"

I nodded through my tears.

"I brought you some lining for it—and here's a size two coat pattern."

That material made the fleeciest, softest, washable white nylon coat imaginable! Ruthie wore it for two years (I always cut ample hems!), and subsequent miscellaneous cousins wore it for years thereafter! I kept the pattern, though, as a reminder that my God cares for me.

There is a God in Heaven who cares about you, too. It matters very much to Him that you have the beautiful clothing you need. He has promised you He will supply it, if only you will put Him first in your life.

Chapter 6

God Wants You to Look Like a Woman

Almighty God, Creator of Heaven and earth, never does anything without purpose. There is design and plan in everything His omnipotent hand touches. Nowhere is this more evident than in His creation of the human race.

"God said, Let us make man in our image, after our likeness. . . . So God created man in his own image, in the image of God created he him; male and female created he them."— Gen. 1:26,27.

This Scripture tells us God purposely created two distinct sexes to fulfill His plan for the family. Then He named them to show their distinct functions.

The male He named man.

This man is created in God's image. He has a formidable task: he is to subdue the whole earth. But God gave this creature of His a strong, competent body and the will to tackle this immense task.

The man is created to be the provider of the home, the protector from danger, the guardian of the family. He bears in his body the life-giving seed. Made in the image of God, he is to be like God to his family.

He is the high priest and intercessor for the home (Job 1:5; Gen. 25:21). He bears the spiritual welfare of the family on his heart. He is to be, like Christ, the lover of his beloved, selfless in his concern for her, willing to give his life for her (Eph. 5:23,25).

The female God named woman.

God created the woman (which means "out of man") not only in His own image, but specifically in the image of the man. She is the glory and crown of the man (I Cor. 11:7; Prov. 12:4). God formed the woman out of the body of the man, not as an afterthought, but deliberately, to show her distinctive purpose and dependence on her husband.

The woman is the keeper of the home. Her body is not designed for keeping wild beasts at bay or felling the forests, but for the sensitive task of keeping the home comfortable and comforting.

She bears in her body the precious, unborn child. After its birth, she suckles it, cares for it, trains it. She is what makes the husband's toil-filled life worthwhile.

Though woman is of the man, and created for him, man cannot exist without her. As a molecule of water must contain both oxygen and hydrogen to be the life-giving liquid essential to man; as a bolt is useless without the nut; as meaningless as a scissor is without its corresponding blade, so man and woman are incomplete without each other. Adam, restless and longing for what he could not image, discovered that Paradise itself was incomplete without someone with whom to share it.

A baby comes into the world endowed with an innate knowledge of its maleness or femaleness. A baby girl is born with the intrinsic emotional patterns she'll need for home-keeping. A baby boy comes into the world with the physical and mental endowments he'll need for guiding a home.

It's no accident that little girls usually reach for baby dolls and that most little boys prefer trucks. God created each little heart and mind so the child would naturally enjoy the kind of activity He has planned for it.

Men, the psychology books say, use their big muscles more efficiently; women excel in manipulative actions, taking care of little things. Men are more efficient handling machinery. Women are usually better in seeing after details. Boys tend to do better in math; girls, in memory and language.

A man must be aggressive if he is to conquer the natural world. So God made him aggressive. Gilbert, a psychologist,

says, "Males are more overtly aggressive from childhood onward, two and a half times as much as females"
(*Encyclopedia of Human Behavior* by Robert M. Goldenson,
p. 1194, article on "Sex Differences").

God seems to have made it easier for the ordinary woman
to do common household tasks than a man.

A woman peeling potatoes uses only 1.29 calories, while
a man peeling potatoes (if you can get him to do it!) uses 2.7
calories—more than twice as much energy.

A woman uses 1.53 calories washing dishes. A man
doing the same task uses 3.3—he works twice as hard. A
woman making a bed uses only 5.4 calories; a man uses 7.

But a man does not spend near as much energy in hard,
outdoor activity as a woman does. God built the man for
tremendous strength and energy. He built the woman for
long endurance. (See page 194 of *The Body, Life Science
Library.*)

These days many psychologists reject this view. They
blame the apparent differences in the sexes, not on intrinsic
characteristics, but say parents mold their children into
stereotyped "roles."

(I dislike the word *role* for expressing the different
responsibilities of men and women because it implies playacting. What we are talking about is not playacting at all,
not an assumption of a personality that can be lightly laid
aside at will. This is an intrinsic part of the personality. But
for want of a better word, I'll use the word *role* as the psychologists do.)

B. F. Skinner speculates on the idea that children do not
naturally prefer male or female roles. In his book, *Walden
Two,* he describes his ideal society. In it, children will be
taken away from their parents at birth so they won't be damaged by wanting to be "like Daddy" or "like Mother"!

In our society, Skinner complains, a little girl is doomed
to grow up to be a neurotic housewife (p. 146, Walden
Two, MacMillan). But, Skinner says, if she has no sexual

identification, she will grow up to be a happy adult!

(You'll take what Skinner says about children with a grain of salt when you discover, later on in the book, that he knows so little about babies he thinks they need to be bathed only once a week if the air in the nursery is properly filtered! Any ordinary, "un-Ph.D.'d" mother could tell the educated doctor that what makes babies dirty is something much more tangible than unfiltered air! If he knows so little about the physical needs of babies, why should we believe he understands their emotional and spiritual needs?)

All levity aside, Skinner's mammoth assault on the home is dangerous. It is a matter for deepest concern by thoughtful Christians. God established the home before any other institution. He has invested parents with the awesome responsibility of rearing God-fearing, productive children. We must not let the psychologists and sociologists wrest this task from us.

In the 1950s, baby specialist Dr. Benjamin Spock counseled mothers to let little boys do masculine things and little girls be feminine, so they would learn to identify with their proper roles in life.

In 1974 Dr. Spock bowed to feminist pressure and apologized for his "male chauvinist" opinions. He revised his baby book accordingly. Why? Not because the facts changed!

Some psychologists now discount earlier studies that indicated children showed a marked preference for traditional male and female roles at a very early age. They were not indicating real preferences, the new psychologists explain; they were reflecting culturally-induced patterns. Mother and Daddy had conditioned their darlings, perhaps unconsciously, by their own frustrated, restrictive behavior. Why did these psychologists change their minds?

Why deny the obvious fact that children often early in life do reveal preferences related to their sex? Why? Because some behavioral psychologists don't like anything that hints a child has an innate moral sense, that a child is born with a certain moral awareness. They would like to think the child is as amoral as their laboratory animals.

Because they reject God, the Creator, they reject the fact that God's creation, the child, bears the imprint of His plan.

There *are* things we know without being taught. There are emotions, preferences, abilities built into us. They are there long before we've grown aware enough to observe them in others and imitate them.

(I forbear to use the word *instinct* to describe this innate knowledge, since scientists use that word in a more restrictive sense. Perhaps the phrase *intuitive knowledge* is better: we know some things without ever having been taught them, without ever having observed them; and we would know them regardless of what culture, what century we were born in. God imprints it in every human heart.)

The Holy Spirit, in Romans 1:18–20, says:

"The wrath of God is revealed from heaven against all ungodliness and unrighteousness of men, who hold the truth in unrighteousness; Because that which may be known of God is manifest in them; for God hath shewed it unto them. For the invisible things of him from the creation of the world are clearly seen, being understood by the things that are made, even his eternal power and Godhead; so that they are without excuse."

We could rephrase this: "Even men who hold the truth in unrighteousness can know certain things about God. God Himself revealed it to them in the creation of the world. They can understand eternal, abstract truths because of the concrete things they can see. A man will be held accountable to know everything that he could know. He has no excuse for being ignorant."

Does this innate, untaught knowledge apply to an understanding of one's maleness or femaleness? Yes, especially so.

First Corinthians 11:14,15 says, "Doth not . . . nature itself teach you, that, if a man have long hair, it is a shame unto him? But if a woman have long hair, it is a glory to her." (We'll talk later about the "long hair" part of this verse; notice for the time being the phrase 'nature itself teaches us.')

Nature itself teaches men and women something about their maleness and femaleness. This "nature" is not the birds and the butterflies: the animal kingdom does not have long or short hair by which to be shamed. No, this "nature" is the innate, inborn knowledge of sexual roles and responsibility that we know without ever having been taught it.

Furthermore, and strangely, it is this innate knowledge that reprobate man rejects. In Romans 1:24 we learn that after men knew God (and they knew Him because of what they saw in His creation, without having to be taught it), they rejected Him. The consequence of their rejection was that their reasoning ability was damaged. They "became vain in their imaginations, and their foolish heart was darkened" (Rom. 1:21).

The result of their rejection of God was that they lost that inborn, innate knowledge of maleness and femaleness. The women became lesbians; they "did change the natural use into that which is against nature" (Rom. 1:26). Men became homosexuals, leaving the "natural use of the woman" (vs. 27).

Jude 10 says something similar: "These speak evil of those things which they know not." There were many spiritual truths they did not understand because their reasoning ability had been impaired by sin. "But what they know naturally, as brute beasts, in those things they corrupt themselves." They did know some things intuitively, and it was in those naturally known things that they specifically corrupted themselves.

It is not an accidental connection: when men reject the knowledge of the power and Godhead of the Creator, they also reject His purpose in creating the human race as man and woman.

This is the source of the radical women's lib movement and the drive by homosexuals for the approval of society. They are both inexorably tied in with the rejection of God's plan for men and women.

No matter what we hear from the news media or congressional inquiries about homosexuality, it is still a wicked sin. It rejects God and His plan for the human race. It is not simply an "alternative lifestyle" choice; it is not simply an aberration to be pitied; it is not a sickness. It is sin.

In God's sight, homosexuality is as wicked a sin as idolatry (Lev. 18:21–30). God invokes the death penalty for it. In Scripture it is always connected with gross rebellion and other wicked sins (II Pet. 2:6–10; Jude 7).

Why is it such a terrible sin? Because it destroys God's plan. It is "confusion" and "abomination" (Lev. 18:22–29).

(Thank God that homosexuality, like every other sin we human beings have committed, can be forgiven. Jesus has infinite compassion for all sinners, and He died so that homosexuals can also be saved and enter into Heaven redeemed and cleansed.)

God intended a man to choose a wife as his mate, to love her and live with her, to establish a home, to engender children and rear them to serve the Lord. Any device of man that thwarts God's marvelous plan is a wicked sin.

"Enough!" you cry wearily. "I believe you. But I thought we were talking about clothes."

And so we are! Here is how all this applies: unless we are aware of God's absolute standard, His different design and purpose for men and women, we are apt to miss the significance of the Scriptures concerning male and female appearance.

Two major Scriptures teach this.

The first is Deuteronomy 22:5: "The woman shall not wear that which pertaineth unto a man, neither shall a man put on a woman's garment: for all that do so are abomination unto the Lord thy God." Each sex is to wear distinctive clothing.

The second is I Corinthians 11, which discusses the order of authority in the universe. Each sex is to have distinctive hair length.

There are thorny problems in both these Scripture passages, and Bible scholars do not always agree on their meaning. Suppose we start another chapter to tackle them, but before we do, let's make one more observation.

When we talk about the role and responsibility of men and women, we are not talking inferiority or superiority. Men and women simply are different.

Nor does this imply a woman can only be a wife and homemaker, that her only purpose in life is to be "barefoot and pregnant, standing at the kitchen sink washing dishes." We are teaching (scripturally, God being our helper!) that if a woman chooses this role, God has clearly outlined her responsibilities.

It's no handicap to be a woman in your relationship with God. We are all the same in the presence of the Lord Jesus. Galatians 3:28 tells us, "There is neither Jew nor Greek, there is neither bond nor free, there is neither male nor female: for ye are all one in Christ Jesus."

The dear Lord Jesus gave His life for the eternal soul of every woman. She is precious to Him just because of herself. When she prays, she has the ear of God as surely as any man. God promised to send His Holy Spirit on His handmaidens as well as His men servants (Acts 2:17,18).

Don't chafe at the position God put you in. He planned it for your joy, your fulfillment. He loves you. He wants you to be happy. He is so wise that He knows what will make you happy. He is strong enough and wise enough to arrange every circumstance in your life to make it right for you.

Why not serve Him gladly within the framework of the body He prepared especially for you?

Ready to tackle Deuteronomy 22:5? Go make yourself a fresh cup of coffee, and let's try it.

If you would like further Bible teaching on the question of a woman's submission to her husband, you might enjoy reading my book, **Me? Obey Him?** *which goes into the question exhaustively (and exhaustingly—have you noticed my talent for it)! It's published by Sword of the Lord Publishers, Murfreesboro, Tennessee 37133, and also available at your local Christian bookstore.*

Chapter 7

What Does Deuteronomy 22:5 Mean?

"The woman shall not wear that which pertaineth unto a man, neither shall a man put on a woman's garment: for all that do so are abomination unto the Lord thy God."— Deut. 22:5.

Apparently this Scripture says a woman is not to wear a man's clothing, and a man is not to wear women's clothing. Those who do are an abomination to God.

Abomination is as strong a word of aversion as you can find. It means "extreme disgust, loathing, abhorrence, hateful, shamefully vile." "Abomination"—that's the way God feels when He sees a woman put on a man's garment or a man put on a woman's garment.

Is this what the verse actually means?

Sometimes it has been dismissed by Christians with the comment, "That's only ceremonial law; that doesn't apply to us Christians."

If it is only ceremonial law, then we not only are not obliged to keep it; it would be wrong for us to impose it on others.

When Christ died, He blotted out the "handwriting of ordinances that was against us, which was contrary to us, and took it out of the way, nailing it to his cross" (Col. 2:14). Verses 16 and 17 say, "Let no man therefore judge you in meat, or in drink, or in respect of an holyday, or of the new moon, or of the sabbath days: Which are a shadow of things to come [that is, they foretold coming deliverance]; but the body is of Christ."

All ceremonial laws were abolished at the cross. All moral laws are still in force. How can we tell if this is ceremonial law or moral law, and therefore binding?

You'll remember that a ceremonial law was established

by God especially for the Jews. It had nothing to do with inherent right or wrong. It involved a certain ceremony (hence the word *ceremonial*) that would teach the Jews something specific about their "set-apartness" for God. Jews were commanded to do certain things just to show they were different.

For example, they were forbidden to eat certain animals and birds. But God changed that command after the death of Christ. In Acts 10:15 God told the Apostle Peter, "What God hath cleansed, that call not thou common." The object lesson had been taught: it was impossible to earn salvation by keeping rules.

The lesson is ended. Now anyone, Jew or Gentile, can eat meat. First Timothy 4:3,4 says men will depart from the faith "commanding to abstain from meats, which God hath created to be received with thanksgiving of them which believe and know the truth. For every creature of God is good, and nothing to be refused, if it be received with thanksgiving."

Is, then, Deuteronomy 22:5 ceremonial or moral law? The whole chapter is a mixture of both. Many verses are obviously moral law. If you see a neighbor's ox or sheep wandering, return it. Conserve natural resources so future generations can eat. Take responsibility in your home for the safety of others. A wife has a right to a fair trial if accused by her husband of impurity. Rape is to be severely punished; so is adultery. These are moral laws.

Four verses in this chapter are probably ceremonial: don't sow mixed seed in a field; don't plow with an ox and ass together; don't mix fibers in woven cloth; do wear a fringe on your clothing.

Now, into which of these two categories does verse 5 fit?

One clue is that the Scripture says a woman who wears men's clothing is an *"abomination unto the Lord thy God."* It is a terrible offense to God Himself when a woman puts on men's apparel.

Does God ever use the expression *"abomination unto the*

Lord" when speaking of a ceremonial law? No. The essence of ceremonial law was that Jews would make certain things unclean to *themselves.* Deuteronomy 14 and Leviticus 11 list a number of things the Jews were to consider an abomination. "He is unclean *to you*" (Lev. 11:7). *"All fowls that creep, going upon all four, shall be an abomination unto you"* (Lev. 11:20). All such prohibitions made to Jews in the Old Testament were canceled in the New Testament.

But when the phrase "an abomination to me," when God is speaking, or "an abomination to God" is used, the Scripture is forbidding a gross moral sin, something inherently and obviously wrong, and equally condemned in the New Testament.

Idolatry is an abomination to God (Deut. 7:25). So are human sacrifices (Deut. 12:31), witchcraft (Deut. 18:10–12), murder, and lying (Prov. 6:16–19; 12:22).

Therefore, when God says it is an abomination to Him when a woman wears a man's clothes, we must conclude it is a moral command, not ceremonial. This sin is in the same class with the gross sins of idolatry, adultery and murder.

In the light of this, many Hebrew scholars believe Deuteronomy 22:5 refers to the heathen practice of using male prostitutes in temple worship, specifically to transsexual "cross-dressing" for deviant sex in the worship of pagan gods. It may be this is its primary meaning.

Any wearing of the apparel of the opposite sex in order to deliberately blur the distinctive work God has in mind for each sex would be wrong. To wear the clothing of the opposite sex might betray (perhaps unintentionally) an unwillingness to submit to the plan God especially designed for each one of us when He created us male or female.

The question that next arises is, "What is men's apparel? What is women's apparel?"

The assumption is that the reader of this Scripture would know which was which. God doesn't ever give a command that we can't obey because we don't know what it means. The second assumption is that men's and women's clothing do differ.

First Timothy 2:9 says, "In like manner also, that women adorn themselves in modest apparel." The word *"apparel"* is the Greek word *katastole*. Young's Analytical Concordance translates it "long robe." (Note, for the moment, that the emphasis is on *robe*. We'll talk later about the *long* robe.)

In this Scripture the assumption is that women will wear robes.

I know of only one situation in Scripture where men were commanded to wear pants. The priests were commanded to wear "breeches" to cover the loins and thighs when they walked up the steps to minister at the altar (Exod. 28:42).

In the I Timothy 2:9 reference, we might ask if God gave this command concerning robes because it was the custom in Timothy's culture for women to wear robes.

Perhaps not. God's Word is eternal. It will last forever (Ps. 119:89; I Pet. 1:23). It is as applicable and relevant to us who live in an urban, mechanized, mobile society as it was to people two thousand years ago living in a rural, agricultural, simple society.

Furthermore, the stress of Scripture is that we are not to conform to the world's standards of culture if they violate Scripture (Rom. 12:1,2). Some of Christ's most scathing denunciations were against those who taught the traditions of men as if they were the doctrine of God (Mark 7:7). God didn't notice that most of the women in Timothy's church wore robes and then determine that all Christian women in that town should wear robes.

In fact, God graciously makes allowance in Scripture for those of different cultural backgrounds in non-moral matters.

The outcome of the Council of Jerusalem (Acts 15) was that Gentile Christians ought not to offend Jewish believers and that Jewish believers ought not to require ceremonial customs of Gentile Christians.

In fact, when cultural customs are referred to in Scripture which might not be familiar to those of another culture, the Holy Spirit often takes time out from the narrative to explain that custom: for example, in Ruth 4:7, "Now this was the manner in former time in Israel concerning redeeming. . .a man plucked off his shoe, and gave it to his neighbour." Second Kings 11:14, Esther 1:13, and I Samuel 9:9 have similar explanations.

God would not ever give a command in Scripture that depended on our knowing about a foreign culture from an external source, apart from His Word, before we could understand it enough to obey it.

Second Peter 1:3 says, "His divine power hath given unto us *all things* that pertain unto life and godliness . . . Whereby are given unto us exceeding great and precious promises." So God's Word does not require light shed on it from secular history in order to understand what is expected of us.

Certainly we are profited by light from other sources on the Word of God. We are enriched by what Bible historians teach us. I speak now only of God's commands themselves being plain.

Whatever I Timothy 2:9 means, it is not just a command to first-century women in their relationship to a local cultural custom. It is for women living today in our culture as well.

The Bible also makes many references to men wearing robes. The Greek word *stole* is used of men's garments as well as women's. Three times the word is translated "long robe" or "long garment."

How can there be a distinction if men and women both wear robes?

A clue is found in the Greek word *katastole*, used only once in Scripture, and there it refers to women's clothing. The Greek scholar says that word means "properly a lowering, letting down, hence, a garment let down." This seems to indicate a woman's robe would be longer than a man's.

Another clue is found in Deuteronomy 22:5. The word *"garment"* is the Hebrew word *simlah.* In contrast to an inner garment or vest, *simlah* means "outer garment." This implies it is the outside, the obvious, the immediately distinguishable garment that ought to differ between men and women. The silhouette, the total impression, is to be distinctly male or female. You ought to be able to tell, at a glance, whether one is a man or woman.

In Zondervan's Pictorial Dictionary, the article on Hebrew women's dress says:

> A few articles of female clothing carried somewhat the same name and basic pattern, yet there was always sufficient difference in embossing, embroidery, and needlework so that in appearance the line of demarcation between men and women could be readily detected (page 227).

In the more remote parts of Arab lands today, where clothing is essentially the same as it was in Bible times, this statement is still true. Though the traditional Arab dress for men and women is the robe, there is never the slightest doubt in your mind as to whether you are viewing a man or a woman. The entire silhouette is different.

One day at the dinner table our children were discussing our paper boy—or was he a paper girl? He wore a shirt and blue jeans—but that proves nothing these days. His (or was it her?) hair was long and curly, with cute bangs. He wore loafers with a fringe. I was inclined to agree with my girls— no boy could have curls that pretty! But my son Paul won the argument. "It's a boy," he said positively. "He rides a boy's bicycle!"

That is what God meant when He described "confusion."

Does Deuteronomy 22:5 then mean a woman ought never wear slacks? In this country most women wear slacks. If most women wear them, doesn't that automatically make them women's apparel?

Perhaps so. But if women's and men's apparel are to be distinct, how can a woman make her slacks distinct from a man's?

Not by color—pastels are no longer the private province of women; color alone no longer conveys femininity.

"My zipper is on the side instead of the front," a woman explained to me. "I made my slacks for me, so you can't say they are man's apparel."

But does that meet God's expectation that the silhouette, the first impression, be distinctly feminine? To tell the truth, you wouldn't be very happy if a man checked to see if the zipper of your slacks was in front or on the side.

"But slacks are so much more comfortable than a skirt," you might say. Your comfort is a subjective matter. You really may be more comfortable in pants, but should we make comfort our first consideration? A hundred times a day we choose to do what is not comfortable—but right. We get out of bed every morning when staying in bed would be more comfortable.

"But slacks are more modest than the skirts most women wear. Isn't it better to wear slacks than to be immodest? Aren't pants the lesser of two evils?"

(In a later chapter we'll talk about whether slacks are more modest than a skirt, and yes, I realize that's the third time I've told you we'll discuss something later. You've no idea how hard this book is to keep organized! Right now, let's talk about whether slacks are the lesser of two evils, mannishness or immodesty.)

Charles Spurgeon said, "When choosing between two evils, choose neither."

Is it better to be immodest or to wear men's apparel? Spurgeon says, "Choose neither." You don't have to choose between immodesty and unwomanliness. You can be modest and womanly.

When we must make a moral decision, let's erase from our possible choices every alternative that involves wrong. If you feel you have no choice but the lesser of two evils, it is because you have not considered all the alternatives.

You do have another choice, somewhere, somehow, so that you won't have to break any of God's commands. He promised in I Corinthians 10:13 to provide a way we can escape from temptation. God always keeps His Word. There is always some way to solve a problem without choosing evil. You may have to do some creative thinking (and perhaps some designing and sewing—I'm not promising you it will be the easy way out!). But you *can* find a garment to wear that is both feminine and modest—and functional.

"But my husband *likes* me to wear slacks," you might exclaim, knowing that I'm the woman that wrote that just-as-difficult-to-handle book, *Me? Obey Him?* You know I believe God wants us to obey our husbands implicitly.

Does he want you to wear slacks because you seem to be more fun, less inhibited, when you wear them? Do they seem to make you more his pal, his companion? That's a gift you can give him, no matter how you dress.

If you are earnestly obeying your husband in everything, not just where your "druthers" coincide with his will, I have a hunch he'll defer to your convictions about this. My husband does not feel as strongly as I do about my not wearing pants, but he treasures my relationship with the Lord and wouldn't want me to do something against my conscience.

"But," you might properly object, "you've taken one teensy-weensy Scripture in the Old Testament and made a federal case out of it. If it's as important as you say, wouldn't God have repeated it elsewhere in Scripture?"

This command is not repeated elsewhere in Scripture. But the biblical principle underlies all man-woman relationships.

Even if it is not repeated, we have to ask ourselves, "How many times must God command us to do something before we obey Him? Twice? Three times? Isn't one clear command enough to show us the mind of God? If we won't listen to Him the first time, would we listen to Him the second or third time?"

Jesus said we are accountable for "every word" that proceeds out of the mouth of God (Matt. 4:4). One command is enough.

Is it "legalistic," rather than living by grace, to obey this particular element of Scripture? I think not. I make choices every day about my life-style to avoid temptation, not to earn God's approval, but simply because He showered His great grace on me.

One of my girls said to me, "But Mother, lots of women don't believe like you do about this, and they are just as good a Christian as you are."

That is absolutely true. I have no corner on God's Word. This is a decision you must make for yourself as you study the Word and see God's heart.

God holds me accountable for decisions I make while reading His Word, regardless of what others believe. Proverbs 22:21 says we are to know the certainty of the words of truth so that we might answer the words of truth back to Him (God) who sent them to us. We are accountable to listen to God's Word, then repeat it back to Him to demonstrate that we really heard Him correctly.

Perhaps the principles given in Romans, chapter 14, for Christians who disagree on certain matters of life-style will help you make your decisions.

First, it is wrong to judge others about spiritual decisions they make as they try to serve God:

"Him that is weak in the faith receive ye, but not to doubtful disputations . . .

"Let not him that eateth despise him that eateth not: and let not him which eateth not judge him that eateth: for God hath received him.

"Who art thou that judgest another man's servant? to his own master he standeth or falleth. Yea, he shall be holden up:

for God is able to make him stand . . .

"For none of us liveth to himself, and no man dieth to himself . . .

"But why dost thou judge thy brother? or why dost thou set at nought thy brother?"

Second, each of us will answer to God alone for our decisions.

" . . . for we shall all stand before the judgment seat of Christ.

"For it is written, As I live, saith the Lord, every knee shall bow to me, and every tongue shall confess to God.

"So then every one of us shall give account of himself to God."

Third, we ought not to give someone else an excuse to sin.

"Let us not therefore judge one another any more: but judge this rather, that no man put a stumblingblock or an occasion to fall in his brother's way . . .

"But if thy brother be grieved with thy meat, now walkest thou not charitably. Destroy not him with thy meat, for whom Christ died.

"Let not then your good be evil spoken of:

"For the kingdom of God is not meat and drink; but righteousness, and peace, and joy in the Holy Ghost."

And last of all, we must not violate our own conscience.

"Hast thou faith? have it to thyself before God. Happy is he that condemneth not himself in that thing which he alloweth.

"And he that doubteth is damned [condemned] *if he eat, because he eateth not of faith: for whatsoever is not of faith is sin."*

This surely ought not be a divisive thing between Christians. A woman's godliness is certainly not determined simply by whether she wears a skirt or slacks. A critical spirit toward others about this would be just as sinful as disobedience in any other sphere.

You might exclaim in exasperation, "But Libby, I just don't like to wear skirts!"

And with that we may have come to the heart of the difficulty. Why don't you like to wear skirts instead of slacks? Is it because slacks are more comfortable? More stylish? Cheaper? More modest? Or could there be a more basic problem of which you are not aware?

Several years ago I was in the library researching a patriotic program I was writing for our Christian day school. Leafing through a yellowed 1933 almanac, I came across a picture of Marlene Dietrich sitting on top of a grand piano, performing in a nightclub. The caption said Miss Dietrich was the first woman ever to wear a man's suit in public. (That was not strictly accurate—history tells us of many women who wore men's clothing.) When asked why she dared to do so, she retorted, "Because I'm tired of men having all the fun in life."

A friend of mine was shopping in one of the largest department stores in Atlanta. She was astonished that they had dozens of racks of pantsuits and only one rack of dresses and suits with skirts. She expressed her surprise to the saleswoman. "You bet," the clerk answered. "We women are finally getting our rights. We're not going to let the men push us around anymore."

Sometimes, then, evidently, a woman will choose to wear pants because she doesn't want the role God lovingly designed for her.

The question, "Who wears the pants at your house?" implies that whoever wears the pants is the boss. God intended for the man to be the leader in his own home.

What you wear does reflect your attitude toward authority.

It reveals how you feel about being a woman. God wants even your clothing to demonstrate that you gladly accept the position He has given you. Your clothing should say, "I enjoy being a woman, and I gladly submit to God's will for my life."

Chapter 8

What Does I Corinthians 11:3–16 Mean?

"But I would have you know, that the head of every man is Christ; and the head of the woman is the man; and the head of Christ is God.

"Every man praying or prophesying, having his head covered, dishonoureth his head.

"But every woman that prayeth or prophesieth with her head uncovered dishonoureth her head: for that is even all one as if she were shaven.

"For if the woman be not covered, let her also be shorn: but if it be a shame for a woman to be shorn or shaven, let her be covered.

"For a man indeed ought not to cover his head, forasmuch as he is the image and glory of God: but the woman is the glory of the man.

"For the man is not of the woman; but the woman of the man.

"Neither was the man created for the woman; but the woman for the man.

"For this cause ought the woman to have power on her head because of the angels.

"Nevertheless neither is the man without the woman, neither the woman without the man, in the Lord.

"For as the woman is of the man, even so is the man also by the woman; but all things of God.

"Judge in yourselves: is it comely that a woman pray unto God uncovered?

"Doth not even nature itself teach you, that, if a man have long hair, it is a shame unto him?

"But if a woman have long hair, it is a glory to her: for her hair is given her for a covering.

"But if any man seem to be contentious, we have no such custom, neither the churches of God."

These verses are the primary New Testament passage that teaches that a woman's appearance should be feminine and also reveal her submission to authority. Like the "sticker patches" of my barefoot Texas childhood, it fairly bristles with questions that require a clear answer if a woman is going to look like God intends.

Verse 3 sets the basis for the rule: "The head of every man is Christ; and the head of the woman is the man: and the head of Christ is God."

The basic theme of this passage is authority. Christ obeys God. Though Jesus is God Himself, He deliberately and totally subjects Himself to God. "When all things shall be subdued unto him [Christ], then shall the Son also himself be subject unto him that put all things under him, that God may be all in all" (I Cor. 15:28). Jesus is our example. By His absolute submission to the will of the Father, He shows us our place of submission: "Not as I will, but as thou wilt" (Matt. 26:39).

As Christ subjects Himself to God, so the man must subject himself to Christ. The woman is to subject herself to the man, her husband, and through the man, to Christ and to God.

Ephesians 5:22 limits that submission. She is to obey 'her own husband,' not every man. A woman chooses the man she will marry, and so she chooses which man she will obey. Even more wonderful, the husband whom she obeys is commanded to love her "as Christ loved the church, and gave himself for it" (Eph. 5:25).

So the emphasis of I Corinthians 11 is submission to authority. The result of submission can be seen in the appearance of the man and the woman. The man's head will be uncovered; the woman's head will be covered.

When a man prays or prophesies, his head must be

uncovered (I Cor. 11:4). Why? Because he was made in the image of God (I Cor. 11:7). A woman is to be covered when she prays. Why? Because she was taken "out of man" and was made in his image (I Cor. 11:8; Gen. 2:21,22). She was created for the man (vs. 9) and as an help meet (Gen. 2:20).

Nature itself—that inborn, intuitive, untaught knowledge that tells a man he is made in God's image, as discussed in chapter 6—teaches a man that long hair would be a shame.

Since the woman was created for the man, she is to have "power" on her head (I Cor. 11:10). The word translated *"power"* is the Greek word for "authority": a woman ought to have the symbol of her submission to authority on her head. A woman's head is to be covered to show her husband's authority over her.

Because of her position, it is uncomely [unbecoming], unseemly, not fitting, for a woman to pray with her head uncovered (I Cor. 11:13). It's a glory to her to have her head covered. Her God-given covering is her long hair.

Why does a woman need a covering?

The answer is not flattering. Since I've promised to be absolutely honest, I have to tell you—gulp—it is because a woman may have defective spiritual discernment (not *always has*, but *may have* if she does not submit to God's authority). She may think she is absolutely right, and still be wrong. (I *told* you it wasn't flattering!)

First Timothy 2:13,14 tells us, "For Adam was first formed, then Eve. And Adam was not deceived, but the woman being deceived was in the transgression."

Eve actually believed the lie Satan told her about the fruit of the tree of knowledge of good and evil. Adam knew Satan lied, but he ate anyway. Why? There was, of course, the element of rebellion against God. But there may have also been a yearning to share Eve's fate, however bleak. In this, he may have been like that heavenly Bridegroom, Christ, who was willing to make Himself sin for us so we could have His righteousness (II Cor. 5:21).

Ever since that fateful day in the Garden of Eden, woman has been prone to be spiritually undiscerning.

We usually think of women being more spiritually-minded than men. After all, the average church has many more women than men in attendance in its services. Also, women probably talk more about their spiritual concerns than men do.

But the sad truth is that a woman may be more easily deceived about spiritual truth than a man. Think of the large number of cults founded by women. The numerical ratio of women to men in cult leadership perhaps surpasses that of any other field—political, educational, or business.

First Timothy 5:11,12 says a woman can easily "wax wanton against Christ" and have "damnation, because they have cast off their first faith." Second Timothy 3:6,7 tells us false teachers will "creep into houses, and lead captive silly women laden with sins, led away with divers lusts, Ever learning, and never able to come to the knowledge of the truth." First Peter 3:7 calls a woman "the weaker vessel," referring perhaps as much to her spiritual frailties as to her body.

But God has made a marvelous provision for a married woman, and that is the loving, wise, compassionate protection of her husband. If she will submit herself to her husband, then she is safe from the most virulent of Satan's attacks.

Ruth the Moabitess said to her kinsman Boaz, "Spread therefore thy skirt over thine handmaid; for thou art a near kinsman" (Ruth 3:9). She was asking him to be her husband, to protect her physically, spiritually and emotionally. When Naomi broached the question of a husband for her widowed daughter-in-law, she asked, "Shall I not seek rest for thee, that it may be well with thee?" Rest would come to Ruth in the arms of Boaz, covered by the skirt of his protection.

We read in the parable in Ezekiel 16 of the God-Man who

rescued the baby girl from death. Verse 8 says, "Now when I passed by thee, and looked upon thee, behold, thy time was the time of love; and I spread my skirt over thee, and covered thy nakedness: yea, I sware unto thee, and entered into a covenant with thee, saith the Lord God, and thou becamest mine."

This orphaned bride had heart-wrenching needs. Her Bridegroom met them all and committed Himself forever to continue meeting them.

This covering and protection means blessing and comfort to the wife, not deprivation or abuse. (To hear us wives complain about it would make you think the opposite, that God had it in for women!)

King Solomon's bride said of her husband: "I sat down under his shadow with great delight, and his fruit was sweet to my taste. He brought me to the banqueting house, and his banner over me was love" (Song of Sol. 2:3,4).

The Hebrew word *"shadow"* is translated other places in Scripture as "defense." This bride felt secure under the shadow, the defense, of her husband.

And notice the banner—the king's symbol of authority—his protection, was not duty, not lordship, not abuse, but love! He loved her! How a wife ought to welcome her husband's protection. She receives it by submitting to him.

Do you remember the story of Sarah and Abraham's journey down to Gerar in a time of famine? Abraham thought his wife, Sarah, was so beautiful that King Abimelech would murder him to make Sarah his wife. So Abraham lied and said she was his sister.

God graciously intervened (as He eternally promises to do) so Sarah, the obedient wife, would not have to go into Abimelech's harem. God warned Abimelech in a dream that he must not touch Sarah.

Abimelech indignantly sent them away with a thousand pieces of silver. He said to Sarah, "He is to thee a covering of the eyes." Abimelech seems to be saying that a husband's protection for his wife is a kind of "blinders." Blinders keep a horse from seeing frightening movements or distractions on the side and shying at them.

So a woman's submission to her husband can keep her single-minded, oblivious to the temptations that might flaunt themselves to a rebellious wife.

With that background, let's go back to I Corinthians, chapter 11. When a woman comes into the presence of God in any kind of spiritual activity, she needs her head covered. God does not want any service from us unless we come with a submissive, obedient heart. "To obey is better than sacrifice," I Samuel 15:22 says. Psalm 40:6–8 says, "Sacrifice and offering thou didst not desire. . . . I delight to do thy will, O my God." Any sacrifice made in rebellion is an abomination to God (Prov. 15:8).

So the woman who wants to please God will have the covering, the sign of her obedience, when she steps into His presence.

Verse 10 says a woman ought to have . . . power (authority) on her head because of the angels.

Angels observe us! What do they see? It may be that a woman who professes to serve the Lord without this covering is as marked as Hestor Prynne with the embroidered scarlet letter on her bosom in Hawthorne's story.

"Because of the angels." This may refer to I Corinthians 6:3: "Know ye not that we shall judge angels?" If, someday, we will judge angels for their response to authority, surely we judges must show our own submission.

Author Larry Christiansan, in his book, *The Christian Family* (page 36, Bethany Fellowship), suggests these angels who look on when a woman prays, may well be fallen angels or demons. If they see a woman praying with her head uncovered, they mark a prime, ripe target for temptation. They know a woman in rebellion against authority will be vulnerable to all kinds of fleshly temptations.

A woman's head must be covered.

Now, we ask, what kind of covering does God intend a woman to use?

The Scofield Reference Bible margin says the covering is a woman's veil. Because there are two different Greek words used in this passage for "veil," some church groups require their women worshipers to wear a hat in the sanctuary.

This idea troubles me when I remember that a woman is not to pray or prophesy with her head uncovered. Could a woman always fulfill this command if the covering God meant was a hat or a veil?

How often in the night, when I am awakened from sleep by a pressing burden, do I pray for God's help about it! Surely God did not intend me to sit bolt upright in bed, clap a hat on my head, then pour out my burden to Him. In fact, if I am really to obey the scriptural command to pray always, my covering must be something that covers me day and night, in every kind of situation, however I am clothed.

Nor is my "prophesying" limited to a formal Sunday school class on Sunday morning. Some of my sweetest opportunities to witness for the Lord come unexpectedly, as I run into a neighbor at the meat counter at the supermarket, poking the packages of ground beef, or as I walk the dog, admire a neighbor's garden and speak to her. And some of my most precious "prophesying" experiences with my children come as I teach them the Scriptures at a serendipitous moment of communication.

It seems to put too narrow a restriction on a woman's "praying or prophesying" if she can do it only while wearing a hat.

If you stop to think about it, what is this whole passage talking about?

Hair! Specifically, hair length: long for women and short for men. First Corinthians 11:15 states it clearly: "If a woman have long hair, it is a glory to her: for her hair is given her for a covering."

Perhaps our next question is, "How long is *long* hair?"

We have two clues.

First, we are told if a woman has her head uncovered, it is just the same as if she shaved her head (vs. 5). Evidently there is no difference in the dishonor of having "shorn" hair or the dishonor of have a "shaved" head. *Shorn* is the past tense of *shear*, meaning "cut." *Shears* are cutting instruments. The opposite of *shorn* is *not shorn*.

A second clue is in the two Greek words translated "covered." In verse 6 the word is *katakalupto*, meaning "covered fully" or "covered thoroughly." In verse 15 the word is *peribolaion*, meaning "covered completely" or "covered all the way around." Here the idea is of fullness, longness.

Of course, there is a wide variation in the natural lengths of women's hair. We cannot be certain that this Scripture teaches that a woman's hair, to be considered "long," must never be cut. But certainly the difference between men and women ought to be immediately apparent in the length of their hair. Men are to have short hair; women are to have long hair.

How short should a man's hair be? Short enough that there be no question that he is a man, not a woman.

Absalom, the son of King David who tried to wrest the kingdom from his aged father, was a real rebel. His long hair was his pride and symbolic of his rebellion. He cut it only once a year (II Sam. 14:26).

In the civil war that followed Absalom's seizing of the throne, he was defeated. He fled on a mule, but his long, luxuriant hair caught in the thick boughs of a great oak (II Sam. 18:9). The mule ran on, leaving Absalom to hang until Joab found him and killed him.

Absalom's hair, the manifestation of his rebellion, caused his death.

Some confusion about long hair for men arises because of the instruction about the Nazarite vow in Numbers 6. A man could make a vow to set himself apart for the Lord for a specific time. At the end of that time, he was to bring an offering to the Tabernacle and shave his head to show

that the vow had been fulfilled. It was to be made for a specific number of days (Num. 6).   Some Bible men were
Nazarites for their whole lives by God's decision: Samuel,
Samson and John the Baptist. Since nature teaches us it is
a shame for a man to have long hair, this vow would shame
him, perhaps signifying the shame Jesus endured on the
cross (Heb. 13:13).

These Nazarites were not showing rebellion with their
long hair, like anarchist Jerry Rubin advocated. He said,

> Young kids identify short hair with authority,
> discipline, unhappiness, boredom, hatred of life,
> and long hair with letting go. Wherever we go our
> hair tells people where we stand on Vietnam,
> Wallace, campus disruption and drugs. We are liv-
> ing TV commercials for the revolution. Long hair
> is the beginning of our liberation from sexual
> oppression.

Once I was at a friend's home where an adult son had
come home to visit. He sported a long, wild and dirty hairdo.
Since he was my friend and knew I loved him, and since I
could see how greatly distressed his parents were, I said to
him privately, "What does your long hair stand for?"

"Nothing, Libby. I just happen to like my hair this way."

"You mean it isn't giving a message of any kind?"

"Not in the least."

"You're not trying to tell folks you don't want to be
considered a Christian?" (I knew he no longer claimed to be a
Christian.)

"Nope."

"And you don't have long hair because all your friends do?"

"No. I couldn't care less what my friends think."

"Wonderful!   If it doesn't mean anything and you don't
care what others think, why not get it cut just for the time
you're home? I'll pay for the haircut! You can see how much

it's troubling your folks. How about it?"

"Never!" he said fiercely—which belied everything he'd said. His long, straggly hair was a symbol of his rebellion.

Did Jesus have long hair? You've seen pictures of Him with long hair, but they were painted from imagination. Some assume Jesus had long hair because they think He had taken a Nazarite vow, as in Numbers, chapter 6. But the Scripture says only that He was a Nazarene, from Nazareth (Matt. 2:23).

Nor was it the culture, in Jesus' day, for men to have long hair.

When my husband and I were in Paris recently, we wandered through galleries of the Louvre where hundreds of statues of Greeks and Romans are displayed. Most of them have decidedly short hair, and the Roman emperors generally had close-cropped hair. Many ancient Roman coins show the same. Museums in London, Rome, Cairo and throughout Israel display paintings and sculptures from Bible times of men with short hair.

There is no evidence anywhere that Jesus had long hair.

"But short hair is prettier than long hair," a woman might say. But that's a value judgment. Others might believe long hair just as pretty. But "pretty" is not the standard. What does God say?

If a woman does wear her hair long, she certainly ought to keep it shiny clean, well-groomed and in a flattering hair style. *Long* and *ugly* certainly aren't synonymous.

"Short hair is easier to care for than long hair," a friend objected. That may be true, though I might build a fair case the other way, noting how many hours a week some hairdos cost my friends. But I don't want to make a choice simply on the basis of what is easy.

When Araunah the Jebusite offered to give King David all he wanted to make a sacrifice to God, David said vehemently, "Neither will I offer burnt-offerings unto the Lord my God of that which doth cost me nothing" (II Sam. 24:24).

I must say, in honesty, that I do not always find long hair

easy to care for. It takes skill and patience to style it so it will be attractive and stay neat. I make no guarantees that long hair will be easier to care for or more attractive. I just say that when a woman sets out to please the Lord, then she knows she has His ear when she comes to pray.

A woman said to me, "But read verse 16. It says, 'But if any man seem to be contentious, we have no such custom, neither the churches of God.' Isn't Paul saying people could argue about long hair if they wanted to, but the women in his churches didn't have long hair—they had 'no such custom'?"

Think about it: is it reasonable to interpret verse 16 in that way, when Paul, for the first 15 verses, and under the inspiration of the Holy Spirit, taught women to have long hair? Is it plausible that he then said, "But that's not what we do in our churches"?

Is it reasonable, especially when, as Paul started this teaching on long hair in verse 1, he said, "Be ye followers of me, *even as I also am of Christ*"? Paul did not reject in his own churches the teaching he had set forth so carefully.

Actually, verse 16 is saying, "If you want to be contentious about it, so be it, but we have no other custom in our churches, nor do the other churches of God."

Perhaps you have come to agree with what this passage of Scripture teaches. You might ask, "But what do I do now, since my hair is already cut?"

The story of Samson, in Judges 16, gives us a clue. An angel from God told Manoah and his wife, before Samson's birth, that a razor must never touch his head. When Delilah betrayed him and had his hair cut off, the Scripture says, "the Lord was departed from him" (Judg. 16:20).

Samson lost his great strength. The Philistines bored out his eyes with a hot poker and set him to grinding in the prison house.

Then Judges 16:22 says, "Howbeit the hair of his head began to grow again after he was shaven." God restored Samson's strength and let him kill more of God's enemies in his death than in his life (vss. 28–30). Evidently, once Samson confessed his sin, the wrong was righted, and God, viewing the heart, was perfectly content with the hair which had begun to grow.

So, it seems to me, if a woman has worn her hair short but decides to let it grow, God would see her heart and be satisfied.

There is a strange and mysterious Scripture in Numbers 5. The chapter tells a man what to do if "a spirit of jealousy" seizes him and he fears his wife has been unfaithful. He is to bring her to the priest. The priest is to make a drink using the dust from the Tabernacle floor. If she has been unfaithful to her husband, God would make the drink a terrible curse: her 'thigh will rot, and her belly swell.' However, if she was unjustly accused, if she was faithful, the poisonous water could not harm her. God would reach down from Heaven to miraculously protect the pure wife wrongly accused.

But notice what the priest does when the woman is first brought to him: "The priest shall set the woman before the Lord, and uncover the woman's head." The Hebrew word "uncover" is actually the word unloose, unpin. The priest first was to let down the hair of the woman's head.

What does this mysterious procedure mean, this unpinning of the hair, letting it fall loose? Is it perhaps that, before the test even begins, Heaven and earth can witness by her hair whether or not this woman has been living in subjection to her husband, faithful and pure? Is that witness to be seen in the "loosened" hair, whether it was long or short?

We sometimes say, "Let's let down our hair," meaning, "Let's be absolutely honest with each other." Could this be a vestige of the ancient rite of the loosening of a woman's hair when she was standing before God?

Oh, when Satan stands before the throne of God and makes accusation against me, as he assuredly does (Job 1:6; Rev. 12:10), and when God bids me loose my hair so my obedience can be seen, what does that High and Holy One behold in me?

Chapter 9

What a Woman Doesn't Understand About Men

My husband and I strolled down a narrow street in Damascus, shepherded by our articulate, eager Arab guide. "Now we will see the fabulous palace of Azam," he announced. When we arrived at the "palace," we saw only a high stone wall of indifferent character, overshadowed by ancient Roman ruins and the minaret of a Moslem mosque.

The guide sensed our disappointment. He flashed a confident smile. "Do not worry. It will be as I promised. Damascus lies in the pathway of every world conqueror. We have learned to hide our precious possessions so they will not be coveted by the invader."

His dark eyes softened. "And that is why our women are veiled. They are our most precious possession, and we do not want the invader to covet them."

We walked through the unassuming gate and stepped into a dream of beauty and grace. The heart of the place was a jewel of a courtyard. In the center a fountain poured out cascades of water. A nightingale sang from a golden cage in a shaded nook. Cloisters flanked three sides of the courtyard, with columns of polished fossils, ceiled with mosaics of turquoise and lapis lazuli and gold. Inside, whole rooms of furniture were fashioned of inlaid mother-of-pearl. It was exquisite beyond imagination. We found ourselves hoping no invader's eye would see, and lust and destroy its loveliness.

Our guide had said, "This is why we veil our women. We do not want the invader to covet them."

At the very beginning of our story we learned that Adam and Eve, in the Garden of Eden before the Fall, were naked and unashamed. But the very first thing they did after they fell into sin was to stitch together garments of fig leaves to cover their nakedness.

Sinless, they had no need for clothing. Sinful, they were naked, ashamed and aware their sinful bodies required covering.

It was in the infinite plan of God that a man and his wife enjoy each other's physical bodies. You have only to read the beautiful, explicit, sensuous passages of the Song of Solomon to know that God intended for a husband and his wife to express their inexpressible love in the marriage act. They become "one flesh" in the act of love. It is mysterious beyond comprehension, especially when we remember that God uses this act of love as His picture, in Ephesians 5, of how much He loves us. There He says, "This is a great mystery" (Eph. 5:32), and so it is.

But the entrance of sin into the world brought with it the contamination of all of God's holy gifts. This relationship, too, this pure love, has been mimicked and fraudulently counterfeited by Satan. He attempts to substitute lust—that passion only for the body, without regard for the spirit of the one from whom it takes—for the infinitely holy love a man ought to feel for his wife. Satan intends to corrupt the marriage relationship every way he can, to void the picture of Christ's death for us, and to make poor sinners think happiness can be found in satisfying the flesh.

Since the Fall, no longer can a woman move in the outside world naked, without shame. Her nakedness might cause a man not her husband to lust after her, and so cause him to sin (Matt. 5:28). A woman can never forget this sad truth when she clothes her body. She walks in a world corrupted by sin. She ought never set afire an unholy desire because she did not clothe herself rightly.

Before we look at some statistics, let me say emphatically and unforgettably that a man never ever has a right to rape a woman, regardless of what she is wearing. There is no excuse, ever, for a man's forcing himself on a woman. Many women have endured the agony of rape when they were absolutely innocent, in their own homes, properly clothed, not at fault in any way. Believe me, this is not meant to make a woman feel guilty for something for which she is not guilty.

But let's take a look at the statistics.

The *Atlanta Journal*, March 3, 1970, ran a survey by Hollywood Social Studies of top law enforcement officials in fifty states. Of those who answered the questionnaire:

- 90% believed girls who wear miniskirts risk increased danger of a rape attack.

- 94% thought statistics showing increasing molestation of young girls might be caused by shorter dresses now being worn.

- 98% said provocative clothing, including short skirts, might encourage men to sex crimes.

- One responder said, "Skirts which allow or give promise of a possible striptease view of intimate areas when seated, may put the wearer in a questionable light, sometimes making her the target of immoral advances or comment, or even a sex crime."

Though statistics on forcible rape declined in the five-year period ending in 1963, they suddenly shot up in 1964, 68% in the United States and 90% in England. One factor, the report said, could have been Mary Quant's introduction of the miniskirt. (She designed it, she said, to announce that she was ready to go to bed with a man anytime, night or day.) The Hollywood Social Studies report concluded, "No other adequate cause for this strange reversal has been found."

It is a fact of life that careless exposure of the female body can incite passion in the male, and sometimes another woman, not the one who exposed herself, is the one who suffers the trauma of that man's passion burning out of control.

This is why in I Timothy 2:9 women are commanded to adorn themselves in "modest apparel, with shamefacedness and sobriety." This verse has all kinds of interesting ramifications that help us understand what the Lord has in mind.

We are to dress in "modest" apparel. The Greek word is *kosmios*: "orderly, becoming, seemly, decent, proper." The word *"apparel"* is *katastole*, which we talked about earlier. It means "long robe" or "lowered, let down."

The word *"shamefacedness"* has more startling implications. It is the Greek word *aidos*, meaning "modesty" or "reverence." It is used only one other place in the Bible, in Hebrews 12:28,29, where it is translated *"reverence."* "Let us . . . serve God acceptably with reverence and godly fear: For our God is a consuming fire." We must serve God with "shamefacedness" because He is a consuming fire. We must not come presumptuously.

Thayer's Greek Lexicon says *aidos* is objective in its reference, having regard to others. This intimates a woman will dress with an awareness of how it affects others. Trench, another Greek scholar, says this sense of shame, or modesty, precedes and prevents a shameful act. A woman ought to dress with "shamefacedness," sensing a responsibility for her effect on others.

Older women are to admonish the younger, Titus 2:5 says, "to be discreet." That is the Greek word *sophron*, "of sound mind." A woman should be intelligently aware of her behavior. "I will therefore that the younger women marry, bear children, guide the house, give none occasion to the adversary to speak reproachfully" (I Tim. 5:14).

A sincere Christian woman conducts herself wisely, aware that a wrong act will bring reproach on the name of Christ.

The Bible phrase often used to describe the sex organs is "the secret parts" (Deut. 25:11; I Sam. 5:9; Isa. 3:17). The sex organs are not shameful. They are holy, part of God's plan for the creation of eternal souls. They ought not be made common and dirty by careless exposure.

In fact, the idea of concealment and virginity are so closely tied together that the same Hebrew word is used for both. *Almah* means "virgin, unmarried female," but it also means "concealment."

So a women does have a solemn responsibility to keep her body well covered. Then why are many women so often careless about it? A woman oftens sits down without ever seeming to be aware that her skirt is awry, revealing her thigh. Or she may sit with knees spread far apart, perhaps because she's accustomed to wearing slacks.

The ushers of a fundamental church once came to their pastor asking him to arrange some way they could take the offering on Sunday mornings without having to look down at so much exposed flesh. The women who offended them were probably devout women who had also come to worship the Lord, but they did not dress so the men could keep their minds on the Lord, too.

I sometimes blush for my sons when I see them suddenly avert their faces in a conscious effort not to see more than they ought in a passing figure.

It isn't just a matter of skirt length. Often a neckline is too deep, a sweater too tight, a fabric too clinging. A dress with wrist-length sleeves, hem-line touching the floor, and a high neckline can still be tantalizingly revealing.

Why are even Christian women careless?

Perhaps because women don't think like men think. God simply did not make their emotional makeup like men's. Since they don't respond to the same kinds of stimuli men do, they may not understand why what they wear can be so provocative.

A woman ordinarily is not sexually excited by visual images. Normally, the sight of a nude male would not move her to passion; it more likely would repulse her.

A woman responds to touch. A man's gentle hands do more to give a wife a sense of total protection and arouse a responding love than any picture could. That's why, in I Corinthians 7:1, Paul said, "It is good for a man not to touch a woman." A man who touches a woman whom he has no right to touch might arouse emotions not easily quieted. So the rule ought to be "hands off" until the right to touch belongs to him.

On the other hand, a man can be aroused by a glimpse. Therefore the lust a man might feel by looking at a woman can be so real that the Lord calls it a sin. "Whosoever looketh on a woman to lust after her hath committed adultery with her already in his heart" (Matt. 5:28).

How very important it is for a godly woman to walk so circumspectly, dress so carefully, and handle herself so that a good man would never be accidentally tempted to sin. You cannot be blamed, of course, for the thoughts of every man who sees you, if you are dressed discreetly and acting properly. But we ought to be very careful not to tempt a godly man who is really trying to do right.

How long should a woman's skirt be? First Timothy 2:9 says it should be "modest," lowered, a long robe. It ought to be long enough to cover the contours of the body whether you are standing, sitting, stooping or walking.

Does that require skirts that touch the floor? Probably not. There is another Greek word *poderes* used in Revelation 1:13 which means "a garment touching the feet." Since God did not use that word in the I Timothy 2 passage, skirt length evidently needs to be only long enough to truly cover the body.

This problem of modesty is a factor in your decision about wearing slacks. By their design, slacks reveal thigh, leg and hip. The lines may accent rather than cover a woman's secret parts, especially in trim, fitted slacks. You may feel more modest in slacks than in a dress, but what is important is what a man might feel viewing the female body in slacks.

Some time ago a Christian leader and I were talking about this. For his daughters' camping and sports activities he felt slacks more modest than skirts.

"But how can your girls fulfill the Bible command to look different from men when they wear slacks?" I asked.

"By their pretty girlish curves," he answered.

But isn't that a good reason for girls *not* to wear slacks?

Perhaps a church youth director, wanting to provide wholesome recreation for his teens, asks the girls to wear slacks because the activity with the boys will be so strenuous that they will have difficulty keeping their skirts down. I might question the wisdom of any activity in a mixed group that would cause that much bodily contact, because of the temptations which come with intimate and constant touch.

A friend of mine, fed up with the pressure others put on her girls to wear slacks, finally said in exasperation, "If a girl can't do it in a skirt, then it's not a ladylike activity, and she ought not do it."

I am unwilling to doom an active, enthusiastic girl to sitting on the porch steps embroidering while boys get to do all the exploring of God's physical world. There are ways to lead an active outdoor life and still be a womanly woman who honors the Lord.

For one thing, the right kind of training helps a girl to automatically take care of her skirt, without her having to consciously think, *Oh dear, I've got to keep my skirt down.* She can be taught to be aware subconsciously of her skirt.

At a Sunday school picnic once, as I ran pell-mell down a hill, I stumbled and skidded, face down, full-length for what seemed like a hundred yards! When I picked myself up and limped back to my friends, my sister whispered, "Libby, not a thing showed! You held your skirt down the whole way!"

Believe me, at that moment, modesty wasn't what I had on my mind. Evidently you can train the subconscious mind to take care of that, if you work at it, and my parents did.

Culottes might be a good alternative. They need to be long enough not to hike up when you throw your leg across the horse's saddle, but not so long as to encumber you. They need to be full enough to be comfortable, but not so full they balloon and reveal as much as a skirt would.

If you cannot buy what you like, you can make them

simply by using a skirt pattern that fulfills your other requirements and taking from a slack pattern the crotch curve and pant leg beyond the center line to the inside seam. Commercial patterns are often suitable.

A third possibility might be to wear slacks with a trim cut under your skirt. They are wonderful to keep you warm in cold weather, and the skirt still preserves a womanly silhouette.

There may be some situations where a skirt is obviously unsuitable, and a ski outfit, wind suit, or snowmobiling suit might be appropriate. In my judgment, the sheer bulk of such an outfit keeps it from being very revealing.

I have ice-skated, roller-skated, ridden horseback, played tennis, climbed medium-sized hills, jumped on the trampoline, played touch football with the kids, ridden the Ferris wheel, biked, and motor-scootered in modest culottes. I've lost my dignity many a time but have managed, I hope, to be modest. There are some activities I have reluctantly avoided, seeing no way to handle them modestly.

But for all that, it has been a marvelous, exciting life, and I have no regrets that I've tried to honor the Lord with my clothing.

While we are talking about modest apparel, does it even need to be said that shorts, bikinis, halters, bare midriffs, hip-huggers, and peek-a-boo blouses certainly aren't!

Some women wear slacks only at home or while working in the garden. They find them more convenient than a skirt which might trail into the dirty scrub water or snag on a rosebush. But if she is embarrassed when someone calls and finds her in slacks, then perhaps it would be better not to wear them at all.

The need for modest clothing governed my husband's and my decisions about swimming in public places. Brief swimsuits, even the most modest ones, cannot cover enough flesh for there not to be temptation to young people. We tried to keep that in mind when planning swimming outings with other teens. Sometimes we were able to find two different coves at the lake. Sometimes we set different swim times for girls and guys. When our family was swimming alone, we were still careful to wear wraps on the beach and didn't sunbathe in public.

Parents and children ought to be modest even in the privacy of the home. Girls probably ought not run around in nightgowns or slips, nor boys in underwear.

Years ago Dr. Benjamin Spock, the baby doctor, recommended a certain amount of nudity in the home so a child's curiosity about the bodies of the opposite sex could be satisfied. But in recent years, Dr. Spock has ruefully come to the conclusion that the average child cannot stand the stimulation of seeing a parent's nudity. If he had listened to the Word of God, he'd have known that years earlier.

God cursed Ham for looking on the nakedness of his father, Noah, and getting sexual pleasure out of it (Gen. 9:20–26). This indicates God wants parents and children to dress modestly to be careful even in the privacy of the home.

There is no need to be prudish. It is not wrong for a mother to nurse her baby before the other children of the family. That's a normal function of motherhood which can be handled with grace and discretion. Diaper changing can be handled in the same matter-of-fact way, neither too casually nor furtively. Simply change the baby's diaper because it needs to be changed.

How can you teach the principle of modesty to your children? Suppose you have a teenage daughter who has outgrown her favorite dress. She asks tearfully, "Why, Mother, why do I have to give up this dress? What's wrong with it?"

You don't have to go into a long, embarrassed explanation of the male sex drive and how men react differently than women. You needn't argue with her. Simply say, "This is what God wants us to do. Someday you'll understand why it is necessary. Whether you understand or not, this is how our family is going to do it, just to honor God. Trust me."

For the same reason, if your husband asks you not to wear a certain dress again, don't press him for a reason. Trust his judgment.   Ungrudgingly do what he asks.   The Lord rewards the kind of thoughtful spirit in a woman that keeps in mind the weaknesses and temptations of others and assumes responsibility for her own conduct accordingly.

This old world is full enough of Satan's traps and snares. May we remember to dress modestly so we do not accidentally cause a good man to sin.

Chapter 10

What a Woman Doesn't Understand About Being Female

In the opening pages of this book we talked about the fact that a woman's clothing can betray her spiritual condition.

It is also true that the clothing she puts on can affect how she feels.

Have you seen a little girl put on her mother's "dress-up" clothes and pirouette around the room? The pretty clothes make her feel pretty.

This is one reason, I think, why the Lord took so much time in Scripture to describe how brides adorn themselves for their husbands. No other experience of life, save salvation, is as lasting and far-reaching in consequence as is marriage. It is right for a bride to spend time and thought in getting her bridal clothes ready. They add to the sense of the importance of the event.

What you wear affects your performance. A schoolteacher friend shared this with me. Recently when her principal decided the teachers could wear pantsuits to school, she invested in a whole wardrobe of pantsuits. She shook her head ruefully, telling me about it. "My students beg me to wear a dress to school."

"Why?" I asked.

"They say they like me better in a dress. They say I act differently when I'm in a dress, and they are more respectful. They say, 'Yes, Ma'am' and do what I tell them to do when I wear a dress."

She mused awhile, then said, "To tell the truth, I'm a better teacher, too. I get three times as much work done when I wear a dress. I stay better organized. I feel more professional."

This was a woman who grew up wearing pants, changed

to skirts only when her profession demanded it, but came to understand that how you dress does affect how you feel.

The *Greenville* (S.C.) *News* carried a picture story in 1975 of a nine-year-old girl who plays football on a YMCA team. The paper quoted her as saying, "Sometimes I forget and just think I'm a regular boy playing football." The article continues: "When Katherine is suited and helmeted, she isn't the only one who forgets she's a girl. She figures half the boys on the YMCA league teams don't know it. And those who do just think of her as one of the boys." Then the article describes how her coach slapped her on the rear, as he did the boys, until he learned to his chagrin that she was a girl.

Apart from the dangers of a girl's playing such a bone-crunching sport with boys, I wonder at the wisdom of letting a girl "forget and just think I'm a regular boy." The uniform, in this case, drastically affected her feelings.

The effect of wardrobe on emotion was impressed on me years ago in a humorous way. My sister Jessie and I were shopping for a dress. I can't remember for what occasion. I only remember that when I saw a darling black crepe, with a feminine ruffle at the neck, I thought it might make me look like a sophisticated young mother instead of my pedantic size 14. (You know how most size 14 dresses look, well, very size fourteenish!) This dress looked svelte and trim and gorgeous—all the things I wasn't.

In the dressing room, I slipped it over my head. It felt very snug. Jessie zippered it up for me with difficulty. I looked in the mirror and suddenly felt like a different woman. Jessie looked at me and laughed, for she could see the emotions of excitement and embarrassment in my flushed face.

It turned out that that froth of a dress was a scant size 10, and it covered almost nothing!

What surprised me was the emotion the experience evoked. For those few minutes, until I could wrestle the dress off again, I felt like a femme fatale, a woman of the world who, by the lifting of an eyebrow, might drive a man mad. It was an uncomfortable feeling, and I was relieved when the dress was back on its proper size 10 rack!

This is, I believe, an important reason for a woman to dress modestly—not only for the sake of those who might be tempted to sin, but for her own sake as well. She herself may be affected by what she wears. (I frankly confess it is not easy to sort out cause and effect. Does she put on a scanty skirt because she feels provocative, or does the skirt bring out her feeling of seductiveness? Perhaps it is both.)

In the Bible, nakedness is often connected with sin. In Exodus 32, the children of Israel made a golden calf to worship. They "sat down to eat and to drink, and rose up to play" (vs. 6).

When Moses came down from the mountain, he saw that the people were naked, "for Aaron had made them naked unto their shame" (vs. 25).

Throughout Scripture there are instances where nakedness produced shameful acts. Whatever the intent of the heart in their stripping off their clothing, the result was sin, then shame. Notice this in II Samuel 11:2; Isaiah 20:4; Revelation 3:18; 16:15. "Uncover her nakedness" sometimes is used to refer to an illicit sex act, as in Leviticus, chapter 18.

Several years ago a woman with whom I had been counseling knocked on my door. I hardly recognized her. Her hair was bleached almost white and shingled like a man's.

"O Nancy," I wailed (that's not her name, of course), "what ever did you do to your hair? I thought you were getting things right with God. What in the world did your husband say when he saw it?"

"He said, 'I ought to kill you'—and he kinda acted like he meant it."

I had let her inside the door by now. "Did he have any reason to feel that way?"

"Sure. You wouldn't believe how many guys at work have

propositioned me. Why, even a black man said to me, 'You turn me on.'"

This was a woman married to a man aiming for Christian service. She had often sobbed out her longing for a closer relationship with the Lord. Could a dyed-hair job make this much change in a woman's spiritual life?

I fumbled for words. "Well, now that you know how it affects men, you'll get it changed back, won't you?"

"No, I'll keep it this way. It makes me feel like going to bed with somebody." She looked at me defiantly. "I have a right not to be lonely."

A woman sets herself up for falling into sin when she chooses hairstyles and clothes that are sensual. They will affect how she feels, and she won't want to resist temptation.

There is a profound truth about women that most women don't know about themselves: they are vulnerable. Their own bodies can betray them.

One day long ago I was driving the girls in my high school Sunday school class to my home for an activity. I heard one girl, whom I'll call Sharon, say to the others, "You know, I just love to put on the shortest shorts I can find, and a long tee shirt so it looks like I don't have anything underneath the shirt, then walk down the street. I just love to see the gleam that comes into the boys' eyes."

"O Sharon," I protested, "please, *please*, don't do that. It isn't fair to the boys."

And it isn't fair.

A man's passion is not a plaything to be toyed with, to be aroused and then frustrated by a woman's whim. It is wrong enough for her to stimulate it accidentally by her carelessness. It would be doubly wrong for her, just for fun, to deliberately provoke that holiest of emotions, so profound and pure that Christ Himself used it to picture His love for us.

"Aw, Mrs. Handford," she answered glibly, "don't you worry. I know how to handle boys. If one of them gets fresh with me, I know how to handle him. Don't worry about me."

"I am worried, Sharon," I answered as earnestly as I could. "You can handle any boy you want to handle, but someday a boy will come into your life that you won't want to 'handle.' Then you'll face real tragedy."

She shrugged her shoulders. "Not me."

But within the year she was the mother of a fatherless baby, going through the heartache of giving up the baby for adoption.

Every woman's body is constructed with certain glands and hormones, certain desires and built-in responses that, when aroused, are stronger than conscience or discretion or will.

TV comedians make a laugh out of the line, "This is bigger than both of us." But there is nothing to laugh at when it makes a pure, starry-eyed, idealistic girl into a shamed, fallen woman with a fatherless baby on the way.

The sex drive, once awakened, is far stronger than you can possibly handle. A godly woman must see to it that her clothing does not arouse a desire she has no right to satisfy. She'll not let herself be maneuvered into situations where she won't be interrupted or where the atmosphere is bound to become intimate. This is why my husband and I never allowed our sons or daughters to go on a date in a car alone; they must always double-date with another Christian couple.

This is also why I don't like to see a married woman go to work in a "one-girl" office. It is nearly impossible to retain a platonic relationship. Eventually her husband will suffer by her comparisons to her efficient, urban boss, who may hold his frustrations in until he gets home. A woman working outside the home ought to be aware that she will be bombarded by Satan's darts.

Again and again, when I have talked to a girl who sobs out the story of her loss of purity, I've asked, "How could it have happened?"

She always says pitifully, "I don't know; I just don't know."

And she thinks she doesn't know. She thinks she was betrayed, forced by circumstances beyond her control. Often it was a boy she scarcely knew. Often, for a married woman, it was a family friend, someone she felt perfectly secure with.

So what really happened? The woman forgot she was female.

Recently I completed teaching the book of Proverbs to my Sunday school class of young wives. As I studied verse after verse after verse that warned young men of the snare of the "strange" woman, the harlot, I got almost irritated with the Lord. Why did God always blame the woman? Surely adultery is the man's fault as often as it is the woman's.

But the record is there:

Proverbs 2:16: *"To deliver thee from the strange woman, even from the stranger which flattereth with her words."*

Proverbs 5:3: *"For the lips of a strange woman drop as an honeycomb, and her mouth is smoother than oil."*

Proverbs 6:24: *"Keep thee from the evil woman, from the flattery of the tongue of a strange woman."*

Proverbs 7:5: *"That they may keep thee from the strange woman, from the stranger which flattereth with her words."*

Proverbs 9:13: *"A foolish woman is clamorous: she is simple, and knoweth nothing."*

Each of these admonitions introduces a whole passage of Scripture warning the young man of the wily ways of a seductive woman.

Now I know, beyond any doubt, that the Bible is the very Word of God. It was written by God Himself, the Creator who made us. So when *He* tells a young man to be wary of harlots, I'd better pay attention, rather than argue with Him about it. Thinking about it long and hard, I came to see that the woman does have a great responsibility for what happens in the man-woman relationship. How she dresses, how she conducts herself, will determine the character of their relationship.

The harlot in Proverbs, chapter 7, met a young man "void of understanding" (vs. 7). She was dressed in the "attire of an harlot, and subtil of heart" (vs. 10). This woman deliberately prepared herself to have an affair. She prepared the bed, the refreshments. She even blasphemously used her offering to God for an enticement to the young man!

But notice especially verse 10: she attired herself in the clothing of an harlot. Any woman who dresses in seductive clothing stands guilty before God for what happens.

What is *harlot's attire*? Any clothing that accents the physical features and calls attention to the secret parts of the body.

Does a man have the right to expect a woman to sell what she advertises? Absolutely. If she doesn't want to be propositioned, then she should not dress as if she were advertising for a proposition.

How does she advertise? The Bible tells us it is not simply by what she wears, but also by body language. Proverbs 6:12 and 13 describe the "naughty person" who "walketh with a froward mouth. He winketh with his eyes, he speaketh with his feet, he teacheth with his fingers; Frowardness is in his heart, he deviseth mischief continually."

The way a woman moves, what she does with her hands and eyes, give a clear message without a word being spoken.

In the book *Body Language* (which makes no attempt to view this from a moral viewpoint) by Julius Fast (Pocket Books), the author quotes Dr. Albert E. Scheflen, professor of psychiatry at the Albert Einstein College of Medicine at New York City. Dr. Scheflen says a man and woman telegraph their availability with gestures that may be unintentional but explicit.

The man or woman may begin to use certain gestures which Dr. Scheflen calls "preening behavior." A

woman will stroke her hair or check her makeup,
rearrange her clothes or push her hair from her
face. . . . These are all body language signals that
say, "I am interested. I like you. Notice me. I am
an attractive woman" (page 97).

When one woman at a gathering wants to get a man
into an intimate situation. . .she utilizes body language that includes flirting glances, holding his eyes,
putting her head to one side, rolling her hips, cross-
ing her legs to reveal part of her thigh, putting a hand
on her hip or exposing her wrist or palm. All of these
are accepted signals that get a message across without words (page 98).

I had tried to teach my daughters, without being able to
tell them *why* I thought it important, to groom themselves
well for the day, so they could then forget their appearance.
I wanted their hair under control so it did not continually fall
over their faces and they would have to keep pushing it back.
After reading this, I understood. Constant grooming gestures cannot help but call attention to the body. What we
really desire is that people we come in contact with be aware
of the spirit, not primarily the body.

Recently AP news service carried a story about Copen-
hagen prostitutes: "A Danish court has ruled that a police-
man can tell from the way a woman walks whether she is
soliciting or not. . . . The arresting officer told the court, 'I
took action only when she was obviously soliciting, and that
was easily determined from the way she walked.' "

The headline over the story asked, "Does the Way She
Walks Tell All?" The answer of the Danish court? Certainly!

For these reasons a Christian woman ought to be cir-
cumspect in every way—in her walk, her conversation, her
mannerisms and her clothing. Otherwise, she may convey a
message that will lead to deeply regretted sin.

Occasionally a woman flirts in a situation she feels is

"safe"—the man is also married, or he is a minister or such an old family friend she doesn't think of him as male. A situation like that can become explosive in seconds, too late for control.

The answer? Don't! Don't ever flirt. Don't ever take advantage of a man's manliness or his gentleness.

Why does a woman insist on wearing short skirts, tight knits, low necklines and seem so oblivious to the stress she puts on others? Can it be she subconsciously invites a proposition to sin? Does she like the gleam of desire she sees in a man's eyes?

It makes no difference *why* she does it. The results will still be tragic:

"Remove thy way far from her, and come not nigh the door of her house: Lest thou give thine honour unto others, and thy years unto the cruel: Lest strangers be filled with thy wealth; and thy labours be in the house of a stranger; And thou mourn at the last, when thy flesh and thy body are consumed."— Prov. 5:8–11.

Adultery may be exhilarating for awhile. It may make a woman feel youthful and alive. But it always has sordid, heartbreaking consequences, often with venereal disease and an unwanted baby on the way. It makes no difference whether the woman initiated the encounter or was swept along by her emotions: the results are the same.

The next three verses of Proverbs 5 (vss. 12–14) reveal the heart attitude that caused the adulterer's vulnerability to temptation: He mourns at the last and says:

"How have I hated instruction, and my heart despised reproof; And have not obeyed the voice of my teachers, nor inclined mine ear to them that instructed me! I was almost in all evil in the midst of the congregation and assembly."

What is the first step down the road to sexual sin and

misery? Rebellion against authority and unwillingness to listen to instruction.

If you find yourself arguing with the authority in your life—your father, your husband, the school principal, your boss, about the length of a skirt or the tightness of a sweater, be warned: it could be the first step down the slippery, treacherous road to adultery and a shattered life. Rebellion against authority eventually leads to plain, dirty, fleshly sin.

The godly woman will realize that her body can betray her. She will remember that she has all the intrinsic emotions and drives that have caused others to sin. So she will dress and conduct herself in such a way that she will not be tempted to sin.

Chapter 11

What Does God See When He Looks at You?

It's a recurring nightmare. I'm on my way to church, or school, usually in a hurry. I look down to discover that I've forgotten my shoes, or worse, my dress. I slink around pillars and hide under benches, grasping at any kind of covering, hoping that no one will notice.

I suppose everyone dreams something like that occasionally. Freud, I'm sure, would imbue it with some dark meaning. But I have a hunch it is something basic and elemental. I believe it reveals a deep-rooted consciousness of spiritual need.

In the Garden of Eden, after Eve had sinned, she knew she was naked and tried to cover herself. It was not just an attempt to hide physical nakedness but spiritual sin as well. Job said, "If I covered my transgressions as Adam, by hiding mine iniquity in my bosom . . ." (Job 31:33). Eve's effort to hide behind fig leaves was an effort to cover sin as well as nakedness.

The truth is, all of us are sinners. Anything we do to try to cover or atone for our sins is a miserable failure.

"But we are all as an unclean thing, and all our righteousnesses are as filthy rags; and we all do fade as a leaf; and our iniquities, like the wind, have taken us away. And there is none that calleth upon thy name, that stirreth up himself to take hold of thee: for thou hast hid thy face from us, and hast consumed us, because of our iniquities."—Isa. 64:6,7.

Just as we know we must cover our bodies, so our consciences tell us our sin must be covered from God. But how can we do it?

Reform, and never sin again? That would not take care

of sins already committed. Try as we may, it is impossible for us to go even a day without sinning again.

Should we do lots of good works to atone for our sin? They are like Eve's crumbling fig leaves. "Therefore by the deeds of the law there shall no flesh be justified in his sight: for by the law is the knowledge of sin" (Rom. 3:20).

Nothing we can do to cover our sin is acceptable to God. "Woe to the rebellious children, saith the Lord, that take counsel, but not of me; and that cover with a covering, but not of my spirit, that they may add sin to sin" (Isa. 30:1).

Jesus told a parable in Matthew 22:

"The kingdom of heaven is like unto a certain king, which made a marriage for his son,

"And sent forth his servants to call them that were bidden to the wedding: and they would not come."

After repeated attempts to get his guests to come, but they would not, the king gave his servants other instructions:

"The wedding is ready, but they which were bidden were not worthy.

"Go ye therefore into the highways, and as many as ye shall find, bid to the marriage.

"So those servants went out into the highways, and gathered together all as many as they found, both bad and good: and the wedding was furnished with guests.

"And when the king came in to see the guests, he saw there a man which had not on a wedding garment:

"And he saith unto him, Friend, how camest thou in hither not having a wedding garment? And he was speechless.

"Then said the king to the servants, Bind him hand and foot, and take him away, and cast him into outer darkness; there shall be weeping and gnashing of teeth."

At first glance, this king seems terribly unfair. After the invited guests refused to come, he sent out his servants to bring in everyone possible to the wedding supper.

The servants obeyed and brought in "good and bad." One man came at his king's invitation, but he didn't have on a wedding garment. The king in fury has him cast into outer darkness. (Isn't there a horrible desolateness to that phrase "outer darkness"?) The poor fellow came at the king's invitation, then got kicked out because he didn't have the proper clothes. It doesn't seem fair!

But then you realize this is a parable about the King of kings who does nothing unfair. God has prepared a feast in Heaven that will satisfy every longing any man ever had. He sent His prophets with the invitation. Many, many people, fools that they are, reject the invitation because they love their own way.

But the Heavenly King yearns to share the exceeding riches of His love. He urges His servants to go out and bring in anyone who will come. Revelation 22:17 says everybody who wants to come, may come. The King is providing everything—the food, the transportation, even the wedding garment. They need only to come.

But they must wear the wedding garment the King provided. Our righteous God cannot bear to look on sin (Hab. 1:13).

The man who rejected the King's wedding garment and came in his own clothes was speechless when the King accosted him because he had no excuse. He had known of the King's requirement and His provision of a wedding garment, but he rejected it. He thought a garment of his own choosing would be sufficient.

But he was cast into outer darkness, cut off forever from light and love.

What garment should the wedding guest have worn? The garment Christ provided. His own robe of righteousness He gives as a gift. No merit is needed by the guest. He has simply to accept the robe and wear it.

Christ earned the right to cover your sins when He took your punishment on the cross. You sinned; you deserved to die (Rom. 6:23). Christ died in your place (Rom. 5:8). So He can rightfully give you His robe of righteousness.

What should your response be? Reject the invitation, as the man in the parable did? He died for his rejection. What should your response be? Oh, take the gift! Take it gladly! Accept the robe of Christ's righteousness!

Isaiah said, "I will greatly rejoice in the Lord, my soul shall be joyful in my God; for he hath clothed me with the garments of salvation, he hath covered me with the robe of righteousness" (Isa. 61:10). You'll then be one of the blessed ones whose "transgression is forgiven, whose sin is covered" (Ps. 32:1,2).

The basic thesis of this book won't make any sense if you do not know God. As you've read, you might have been thinking, "What an odd assortment of old-fashioned ideas this gal has!"

Unless you are a child of God and honestly want to please Him, you'll see no need to avoid tempting others by the way you dress. You may not be happy in a womanly role, and you surely wouldn't want to be identified with Christ's team.

But this all falls into place when you come to see you are a sinner in God's sight, with no hope of covering your sin by yourself. Then you will welcome the covering God provided for you in the death of Jesus Christ and receive the gift available just as a gift for the asking. This transaction, this getting the garment of salvation, is as specific and definite as when you reach for a jacket and put it on.

Trusting Jesus as your Saviour makes you God's child. Since God made you and loves you, He wants you to be truly happy. He knows what will make you happy. The principles He has given for your clothing are for your protection and joy, not to make you miserable. Following them will make you a radiant, enthusiastic Christian, not a dispirited, colorless zombie.

But obedience must always precede joy. "If ye know these things, happy are ye if ye do them" (John 13:17).

Are you clothed in the dirty, matted garment of your sin? Or are you clothed in the iridescent beauty of Christ's righteousness? Someday you must give an answer to God's question, "Where is your wedding garment?" Are you suitably clothed against that day?

Chapter 12

What Makes You Truly Beautiful?

Suppose I said, "I have a magic lamp you may use for three wishes. You may change anything about your appearance you'd like to change." In three seconds flat you'd take my offer and make your wishes almost without thinking about it. You already know what physical characteristics you don't like in your own body.

One psychologist reports that when he surveyed teen groups, consistently the girl voted most beautiful by her classmates had a long list of things she didn't like about herself. Why? Because not one of us is really satisfied with the way we look.

That probably becomes more true as we grow older and time ravages our bodies. When our daughter Margaret was 13, she earnestly said to me, "Mother, I don't want to hurt your feelings or anything, but have you seen the advertisement on television for wrinkle cream, and do you think it might help you?"!

As the years go by, we fight crows' feet around our eyes, puddles of fat under our chins, age patches on our skin and gray hairs that stubbornly corkscrew their way through our carefully arranged hairdos! These bodies will age. They are doomed for the grave. We mourn the youthful beauty lost and hope by the magic of cosmetics and careful dressing to camouflage time's inroads.

So how can you explain all the commotion Sarah made when she was ninety years old (compare Gen. 12:17 and 20:2)? A commotion she certainly did make! We're told in Genesis, chapter 20, that Abraham went down to live in Gerar. Afraid the king would covet his wife, Sarah, because she was so beautiful, Abraham told King Abimelech Sarah was his sister.

I can understand Abraham's thinking Sarah beautiful.

After all, she was very dear to him.   But why would Abimelech think a ninety-year-old woman beautiful? For he certainly did!   When he saw her, he coveted her, just as Abraham had feared, and took her to his harem. In fact, God had to intervene with a miracle to rescue poor, obedient Sarah (I Pet. 3:6), to keep Abimelech from making her a concubine.

What was it that made Sarah so desirable?   It wasn't simply that people lived longer in those days, so aged more slowly.   When God told Abraham she would bear a child, Abraham reminded Him that she was too old for child-bearing—she'd already passed through menopause (Gen. 17:17). Nor was it simply that Abraham was wealthy enough to afford jewels and makeup for his wife.

First Peter, chapter 3, gives us the answer.

"Likewise, ye wives, be in subjection to your own hus-bands; that, if any obey not the word, they also may without the word be won by the conversation [behavior] of the wives;

"While they behold your chaste conversation coupled with fear.

"Whose adorning let it not be that outward adorning of plaiting the hair and of wearing of gold, or of putting on of apparel;

"But let it be the hidden man of the heart, in that which is not corruptible, even the ornament of a meek and quiet spirit, which is in the sight of God of great price.

"For after this manner in the old time the holy women also, who trusted in God, adorned themselves, being in subjection unto their own husbands:

"Even as Sara obeyed Abraham, calling him lord: whose daughters ye are, as long as ye do well, and are not afraid with any amazement."

From this we learn a woman's adorning is not primarily her fancy hairdo or ornate garments or expensive jewelry.

Her adorning ought to be the "hidden man of the heart, in that which is not corruptible, even the ornament of a meek and quiet spirit, which is in the sight of God of great price."

A gentle, sweet, quiet spirit is a better adornment than the most elaborate of clothing or jewels.

The specific example the Lord uses is Sarah, who "obeyed Abraham, calling him lord." Sarah's beautiful countenance came from her inner quiet, and it transcended the ravages of the years and desert wind and heat.

First Timothy 2:9,10 says,

"In like manner also, that women adorn themselves in modest apparel, with shamefacedness and sobriety; not with broided hair, or gold, or pearls, or costly array: But (which becometh women professing godliness) with good works."

Good works—happy, joyful service—are a woman's greatest beauty.

A woman cannot make herself beautiful simply by ornamenting her body. Her actions, her spirit are her real adorning. There ought to be a gentleness, a kindliness in a woman of God which permeates everything she does.

In Psalm 45, "a song of loves," we read of the king who will greatly desire the beauty of his bride because "the king's daughter is all glorious within" (vs. 13). She has on golden clothing and raiment of needlework, but her glory comes from within, her heart.

The virtuous woman in Proverbs 31 wore beautiful clothing, but that was not what made her beautiful. "Strength and honour are her clothing" (vs. 25). "Favour is deceitful, and beauty is vain: but a woman that feareth the Lord, she shall be praised. Give her of the fruit of her hands; and let her own works praise her in the gates" (Prov. 31:30,31).

We have no idea whether the Proverbs 31 woman was beautiful or not. Now, three thousand years later, it makes no difference. But her joyful, faithful service is recorded forever in the eternal Word of God.

We can't work up this inner beauty. Standing in a mirror and practicing a "million-dollar smile" won't help. Gluing a patch over the frown lines of your forehead (as a friend of mine once did) can't solve the problem of what put the frown there in the first place. This is not simply putting mind over matter so that you are automatically and magically beautiful. Oh, no. This beauty comes from looking at something—Someone—beautiful.

Psalm 90:17 exhorts, "Let the beauty of the Lord our God be upon us." Psalm 34:5 says, "They looked unto him, and were lightened: and their faces were not ashamed."

Wisdom, that personification of the Lord Jesus in the Proverbs, will "give to thine head an ornament of grace: a crown of glory" (Prov. 4:9).

In the story of the man who found the abandoned baby in Ezekiel 16, verse 14 says, "And thy renown went forth among the heathen for thy beauty: for it was perfect through my comeliness, which I had put upon thee, saith the Lord God."

Moses went to the top of Mount Sinai and there talked with God face to face. There have been many prophets, but never, says Deuteronomy 34:10, "a prophet since in Israel like unto Moses, whom the Lord knew face to face."

When Moses came down from the mount, he "wist not that the skin of his face shone while he talked with him." Communion with God had put a glow on the face of Moses so entrancing that he had to veil it when he talked with others (Exod. 34:29, 30, 33).

And so it should be with us: "But we all, with open face beholding as in a glass the glory of the Lord, are changed into the same image from glory to glory, even as by the Spirit of the Lord" (II Cor. 3:18).

What matter the crooked teeth, the acne-scarred skin,

the swollen, arthritic hands? If you want to be truly beautiful, look into the face of the dear Lord Jesus, then reflect His love and compassion to a world that will die if it does not see Him—in us!

What God Wants From You More Than Anything Else

The world-weary man sat alone in a booth in a restaurant, picking at the plate before him, hungering for something. He was a highly successful businessman, but somehow life didn't seem worth living. During the seventies' protests about Vietnam, he'd gone to jail with other student rioters. Now even that didn't seem very important, not with the truly terrible things that were happening in the world.

Then he became aware of two young, animated voices in the booth behind him. Two college coeds were discussing—what was it? the eavesdropper wondered—about whether or not it was a sin for a woman to wear pants? He frowned and shook his head.

"I can't see it's a big deal," one girl said fretfully. "I keep the rules because I signed a pledge when I enrolled in the university. But I sure know lots and lots of good Christian women who wear slacks all the time, and they sure don't feel guilty."

The other girl answered, "But it's a sin for girls to wear pants, and it makes God angry."

Pants? he thought, *a woman wearing pants makes God angry? And with the whole world drowning in misery and evil, God spends His time worrying about pants?*

The man stood up, picked up his tab and walked away, still wondering at what he'd heard. Here the world was about to blow itself into oblivion, and two apparently intelligent college kids were arguing about something as unimportant as what a woman wears!

Shortly after that, the man, in God's mercy, came in contact with one of the pastors of our church and eventually came to know Christ as his Saviour.

If ever Christians ought to be focusing on the truly important things, surely now is the time! And what are the truly most important things in life? What is it that most concerns our Heavenly Father? The eternal souls of His creatures! He is not willing for one single person in this world to go to Hell. He yearns for every one of His creatures to go to Heaven and be with Him. How holy we live our lives, how attractive we make the Gospel to pagans—those are the truly important things in life.

Twenty years have passed since I wrote this book. Is it still relevant?

There is one teaching in this book which can be legitimately questioned because of current cultural standards, and that is whether pants can still be considered only men's apparel. There are probably many more American women living today who have never worn a skirt, who don't even own a skirt. It could be reasonably argued that pants are no longer exclusively male attire.

It is interesting, still, in this current culture, that on international signs on public rest rooms, the woman wears a skirt and the man pants, because that is the simplest way to distinguish the sexes.

Since this book was written, we have seen an increasing norm of blatant nudity on the stage, in the media and in personal lives. In this respect, I believe godly women would agree that regardless of the current culture, nudity is wrong, and the reminders in this book are valid.

The increased blurring of lines between the sexes, the demands of transvestites, homosexuals and lesbians for recognition and extraordinary privileges—these make the emphasis on God's plan for the sexes, male and female, perhaps more important today than when this book was first written.

But in all honesty, I wrote these chapters on the importance of feminine and modest dress with real trembling for two reasons.

First, I fear a kind of "step-on-a-crack-break-your-mother's-back" legalism which attempts to earn God's favor by keeping an intricate list of *dos* and *don'ts* that of themselves cannot produce true godliness. I do believe the infinite grace of God lavished on us gives us security and joy and helps us to make right life-style choices. "Made free from sin, ye became the servants of righteousness" (Rom 6:18).

Second, I have seen that occasionally a woman, having accepted these truths, will demonstrate a critical spirit toward others who do not hold them.

Many churches have been torn apart by factions of women carping at each other about what appropriate dress is for a woman. The essential work of God has sometimes been hindered by women who felt so strongly about it they have been contentious, thinking they were pleasing God by being contentious. But to cause division among believers about clothing misses the whole point.

A pastor's wife once said to me, "Yesterday a young girl dared to come to our church service wearing a miniskirt. She sat on the very front row, too, where my husband could look at her and be tempted. I gave her real dirty looks so she won't come back again!"

I wept as I listened. That poor girl needed spiritual help. She worked up courage enough to come to church and overcame the embarrassment of having to sit on the very front row of the church, just so she could hear the precious Gospel preached.

What did she meet when she arrived?

Not loving concern for herself as a person.

No welcome to her hungry heart seeking to hear about God's grace.

No, what she met was angry stares, deliberately aimed at her by the pastor's wife so she would not come back. Instead of loving concern, she met hatred. What a travesty of God's grace!

The whole point of this book is that we *not* focus on the

outward, but on the heart. Don't look at the clothes or lack of them. Don't be diverted by the heavy makeup or the irritating mannerisms. Look at the face and see into the hungry heart. See that deep, deep need and ask God to help you meet that need.

How can that girl learn Christ died to save her if she is turned from the church? How can she reform her life-style before she can attend and hear the Gospel? Surely the bitter, hateful spirit of the Christian woman broke the heart of God far more than the girl's short skirt.

We are to give the blessed Gospel to sinners as they are, not as we wish they were. We can hate the garment "spotted by the flesh" and still have compassion, and save them from Hell (Jude 22,23).

The principles of dress are only one small part of our purpose in being on earth: the one important thing is that we so live that people are drawn to Jesus.

"Walk in wisdom toward them that are without [the unsaved], *redeeming the time. Let your speech be alway with grace, seasoned with salt, that ye may know how ye ought to answer every man"*—so you can bring them to Jesus.— Col. 4:5,6.

I beg you, if you have standards and convictions about how a Christian woman ought to dress, let it not be a divisive thing between you and other good Christians who are also trying to serve the Lord.

And may we focus our eyes not on the physical things of this life, but on the "eternal weight of glory." The things you can see—houses, land, even clothes—are temporary. The eternal, important things are invisible.

O God, help us to concern ourselves with the things You say are important: eternal souls for whom Christ died!